R.L.Cousens jr.

12-2-69

Reality in the
Stock Market

Reality in the
Stock Market

Rodger Bridwell

66848

Winfield Press

FOR KATHERINE

I

Acknowledgement

Several chapters of this book first appeared in slightly different form in Barron's National Business and Financial Weekly and are reproduced herein with their permission.

II

Foreword

The traditional approaches to investment management are obsolete today. High taxes, a currency that is depreciating, a debased coinage, inflated prices and lower return on invested capital are all responsible. Before World War II a married couple who retired with $50,000 could live comfortably on the income. Today, savings of at least $250,000 would be required to maintain the same living standard after taxes. *Yet, it is not appreciably easier to accumulate a dollar in the stock market today than it was half a century ago.* If you wish to accumulate $250,000 out of your income you must save $10,000 a year *after taxes* for 25 years. Needless to say, few people earn enough to save this kind of money after paying income taxes, at mid-century confiscatory rates.

Today then, the person who sets out to invest in common stocks must adopt a more aggressive approach than was necessary in the past. Yet at the same time he must avoid following outmoded and highly risky methods of making money. Investment principles that worked in the past don't work today. Traditionally conservative approaches are now often dangerously speculative as will be shown later on. The tax load, of course, must be reduced by striving exclusively for long-term capital gains.

Today's investor cannot be content with a return of 3%, 5%, or even 10% on his capital. He must systemat-

III

ically blueprint and follow a plan that will assure him an average gain of at least 20% or 25%, each and every year. He can no longer invest for income, not even tax exempt income. He can no longer try to beat the market by trading. High taxes together with other disadvantages effectively prevent successful short-term speculation.

"But," you may ask, "Isn't a return of 20% annually on my capital an unrealistically high goal to try for?" Emphatically, NO! At least not if the principle of correct investment procedure is religiously followed. The word "principle" is used in the singular because there is only one way to make money in the stock market year in and year out—and that is by the method blue-printed in this book. (And it might be added, the method followed by most professional investors).

Let's assume by following our plan you do realize 20% or 25% annually; how long will it take an investor with a small amount of capital to build it into a modest fortune? The answer is about 15 years based on annual appreciation of 20% and 25% (without and with reinvesting dividends). Let's say you can begin with an original investment of $5000. Here are the actual figures.

ANNUAL APPRECIATION *

Year	(1) 20%	(2) 25%	(3) 25%**
	$ 5000	$ 5000	$ 5000
1	6000	6250	7250
2	7200	7812	10,063
3	8640	9765	13,578
4	10,368	12,206	17,973
5	12,442	15,257	23,466
6	15,930	18,881	30,333
7	19,116	23,514	38,916
8	23,038	29,392	49,645
9	27,646	36,740	63,056

IV

Year	(1) 20%	(2) 25%	(3) 25%**
10	33,286	46,925	79,820
11	39,943	58,656	100,775
12	47,931	73,070	126,969
13	56,518	91,312	159,611
14	67,821	114,152	190,514
15	81,385	142,690	239,143

* To the nearest dollar.
** Assuming $1000 is added to the account each year—all figures rounded to nearest even dollar.

Now the minimum results shown in columns 1 & 2 are possible without adding a single dollar in savings to the original stake of $5000. However, since most of us manage to save some part of our income, in actual practice at the end of 15 years the retirement fund may well be substantially larger than the figures shown in columns 1 and 2. Thus, column 3 reveals the increase in the final fund if in addition to the original $5000 you manage to save $1000 a year and add it to your investment account.

The key to unlocking this 20%, 25% or even greater annual gain sounds so unoriginal that you may scoff at first. But please be patient. The entire concept is foreign to almost all investors except for the most sophisticated professionals.

The answer, briefly, is to concentrate your capital in companies that are about to make or are in the process of making a UNIQUE PROFIT BREAKTHROUGH. That is, in stocks where a fundamental change has occurred that will soon boost earning power to a permanently higher plateau.

First, we will examine the psychology required before one can hope to succeed in the stock market: Because the investor who lacks the right motives and emotional maturity is certain to fail in the long run.

Second, a number of traditional, widely accepted approaches to investing in stocks are examined at length and discarded as being unrealistic today.

Finally, we will see step by step how to go about selecting authentic UNIQUE PROFIT BREAKTHROUGH stocks and then how to determine when, if ever, they should be sold.

The first step toward success is to face reality.

Contents

CHAPTER 1

Reality vs. Illusion

Reality vs. Illusion—this is the problem. In Wall Street there is a great scarcity of the former, an abundance of the latter. Investors, like other people, believe what they want to believe and it is seldom reality. If the truth disagrees with their selfish desires it is the truth that must be ignored, not the illusions.

The key to making money in the stock market is to faithfully follow a realistic, concrete plan of action. This book outlines a plan based on reality and reality reveals that there is only *one* correct approach to investing in common stocks.

If you don't know precisely what you are trying to accomplish, you are lost. True, many investors will say they are in the market "to make money" and they don't care how they do it. But the "how" is the most important key to success, and success can come only to those who apply positive thinking and emotions to the problem.

Successful investing is relative—never absolute. It varies with the investment or speculative aims of each individual or institution who buys and sells stocks. Consider the speculator. Theoretically absolute or ultimate success would mean holding, at all times, the one stock out of thousands that has gained the most. 100% success would mean all transactions were profitable, no losses were taken. Obviously, such a result is not possible for mortals.

Zero success would mean that all transactions were unprofitable. While we have never known a person who achieved 100% success, we have seen many who came at least close to zero success. Why? These unsuccessful people would give a thousand different reasons for their losses. In fact, any reason except the one real reason.

Among these false reasons are "they" who diabolically make a stock go down after our unsuccessful speculator buys. Or, his broker doesn't know his business and advised him to buy when he should be selling. As a result, he is now "locked in" waiting to "get out even." Or, perhaps, his advisory service was bearish when it should have been bullish or vice-versa. Or, he simply has "bad luck."

The true reason for failure? It lies more or less dormant within each of us.

It is the WILL TO FAIL.

This will to fail is activated by *negative* emotions and thoughts. In contrast the WILL TO SUCCEED is activated by *positive* emotions or thoughts.

If we permit ourselves to succumb to negative emotions 90% of the time, 90% of our market transactions will result in losses. If we are guided and motivated by positive emotions 90% of the time, 90% of our market transactions will result in profits. If our emotions are 50% positive—50 negative, we can expect our investment results to be the same.

In physics this law of nature is known as the Law of Action and Reaction. For each action there is an equal and opposite reaction. Even in the physical world this relationship is seldom obvious to us. Yet it is true, and while today's negative emotion may not produce its retribution until next month or next year or even longer, the consequences cannot be escaped.

Unfortunately, the negative emotions are the instinctive creature emotions and we must constantly battle to overcome them. This is why the stock market baffles so many people. The very instincts which have enabled the human race to evolve to its present material state, assure failure when applied to the stock market. Action that appears to be most logical turns out to be folly. These instinctive negative emotions that must be replaced with their equal and opposite positive emotions are listed below.

Negative Emotion	Positive Emotion
Pride	Humility
Greed or Envy	Charity
Fear	Courage
Laziness	Diligence
Impatience	Patience
Despair	Cheerfulness
Pessimism	Optimism
Selfishness	Unselfishness

Consider the first emotion listed: The person who hasn't the humility to admit his mistakes is headed for nothing but trouble in the stock market. And when that trouble arrives in the form of losses the person who hasn't the humility to accept them gracefully will not have the positive attitude needed to recover and more than recover the losses.

Pride turns illusion into reality and reality into

illusion. The proud, self-centered person acts in a way that will bolster his ego without regard to the consequences. He is more concerned with outward appearances than with positive results. Pride destroys one's ability to choose the correct action. Humility more certainly leads one to the correct action.

To succeed you must eliminate the possibility of failure from your mind. Confidence and faith in the future are necessary virtues. No skeptical, cynical man has ever made and kept a fortune in the stock market. All the famous bears of market history died broke.

Before you can succeed you must first know yourself and then master your emotions. Only character and courage can overcome the twin evils of greed and fear that lead to failure. Unlike most undertakings in a gregarious world, it's a lonely battle because failure can be blamed only on yourself. Only the truly self-reliant *individual* will actually build a fortune. Collective decisions—like all collective action—result in mediocre results at best.

Ralph Waldo Emerson summed up the principle involved in these immortal words:

"The Dice of God are always loaded. The world looks like a multiplication table or a mathematical equation which, turn it how you will, balances itself. . . . Every secret is told, every crime punished, every virtue rewarded, every wrong redressed, in silence and certainty. What we call retribution is the universal necessity by which the whole appears wherever a part appears."

"A wise man will extend this lesson to all parts of life, and know that it is the part of prudence to face every claimant and pay every just demand on your time, your talents, or your heart. Always pay; for first or last you must pay your entire debt. Persons and events may stand for a time between you and justice, but it is only a postponement. You must pay at last your own debt. If you are wise, you will dread a prosperity which only loads you with more."

In short, before we can recognize reality (or truth) in the stock market we must first recognize it in ourself.

If you are dealing in stocks as a short-cut to getting something for nothing, *i.e.,* money without working—forget it or reread the above quote from Emerson: You must pay in full for everything you get.

In the words of a great speculator—Bernard Baruch—who lived in an era when confiscatory taxes were unknown and consequently "trading" was feasible for the gifted few:

"If you are ready and able to give up everything else, and will study the market and every stock listed there as carefully as a student studies anatomy, and will glue your nose to the ticker tape at the opening of every day of the year and never take it off till night; if you can do all that, and in addition have the cool nerves of a gambler, the sixth sense of a clairvoyant and the courage of a lion—you have a Chinaman's chance."

The same reasoning applies when investing for long-term capital gains. Before buying a stock you should investigate the company as thoroughly as though you were about to purchase 100% ownership of a small business. In the latter situation you would probably spend many days investigating every aspect of the operation. The same should be done before buying a stock. Yet, unfortunately, all too often shortcuts are taken in an effort to find an easy path to wealth. Beware of such alluring shortcuts.

In this connection, there must be as many different illusionary approaches to investing in stocks as there are stock brokers and investment advisors—*and* people who write books about the stock market.

Let's look at some of them. Let's try to distinugish between reality and illusion. First in the half truths that are contained in the legendary maxims of the investment community and then in the more specific systems designed to solve the problem of investing in the stock market.

CHAPTER 2

Advice from the Past

The illusionary lore of Wall Street abounds with market
maxims which have been handed down from one generation to the next. And there are a few new ones which have
been coined in recent years to cover situations which
presumably presented no particular problem in the good
old days. The investor who is actually influenced by any
of these or who uses them as a crutch to help him make
decisions had better have plenty of luck—he'll need it.
They all have a small degree of truth but an even smaller
degree of reality, when it comes to practical application.

One of the oldest adages counsels: "Cut your losses, let
your profits run."

This is like saying "Buy only those stocks that are going
to go up." Obviously a desirable rule to follow but how do
you actually do it? One school of thought has come up
with the *10% Rule* for cutting losses which currently
enjoys quite a vogue. (Apparently no one has yet manufactured a simple rule for taking profits). The 10% rule
is simple enough. It simply calls for selling out any time a
stock declines 10% below the purchase price. The rule
must have been discovered by a broker because it will
make a broker rich while it's breaking the customer.

15

Why? Well, a study of market movements reveals that over the years secondary reactions in bull markets have receded an average of 11% from the previous top. Since a reaction of 11% is the equivalent to 15–25% in individual stocks, the 10% rule seems tailor-made to whipsaw investors who hope to "let their profits run" as well as cut their losses short. Here we have an attempt to replace judgment with a mechanical substitute in an effort to escape reality.

The only time the rule will "work" is during the early stages of a bear market (for those investors who try to sell out before bear markets). Yet even here it's effectiveness is limited since anyone astute enough to recognize the beginning of a bear market is probably astute enough to sell out much closer than 10% to the top.

Clearly *unless the reasons for buying a stock in the first place have changed,* the mere presence of a paper loss hardly seems sufficient reason to throw good stocks overboard. On the contrary, reality tells us that if the reasons for buying are still valid, a stock offers better value at 36 than at 40. Only among the illusions of Wall Street would such a proposition need be defended.

We repeat, unless the favorable factors which prompted you to purchase a stock in the first place no longer apply, selling just for the sake of selling can turn out to be a costly practice. Assume a speculator plans to "cut his losses, and let his profits run" by formula. He will sell if a stock declines three points or advances 12 points. This looks good on paper and does have one definite advantage: The trader knows in advance exactly what action to take at all times. But, an important disadvantage is often overlooked. In this example he could be wrong about three times (after expenses) out of four without losing money. But the odds of a three point move down before a 12 point move up are several times greater than 3 to 1. In short, the sum of several small losses may exceed one large profit by a wide margin.

Another ancient adage advises: "Never sell a dull market short." (This would be a worthwhile piece of advice if it simply read "Never sell the market short"). The idea here is that when volume falls off the market is due to rally. As usual this turns out to be right about 50% of the time. Major advances, to be sure, usually get underway when volume of trading is light. However, so do serious market breaks. The stock market collapses which started in August 1937, May 1940, August 1946, and April 1962 are among those which come to mind.

Way back in 1909, William Peter Hamilton observed: "One of the platitudes most constantly quoted in Wall Street is to the effect that one should never sell a dull market short. That advice is probably right oftener than it is wrong, but it is always wrong in an extended bear swing. In such a swing the tendency is to become dull on rallies and active on declines."

Another old slogan—"You will never go broke taking a profit"—Sounds especially convincing to the market newcomer, who can seldom resist taking small profits. If this line of reasoning ever had merit it has long since been rendered obsolete by the tax collectors.

As a matter of fact, following this sort of investment philosophy will break you in the end as surely as night follows day. The simple fact that you have a profit in a stock is a powerful argument for holding rather than selling. By definition a stock that is destined to move up 300, 500 or 1000% over a period of years will almost always be held at a profit. Never surrender a profitable position in a stock that is rising on the strength of a UNIQUE PROFIT BREAKTHROUGH unless you are *certain* that you can replace it with another stock with an even better UPB story; or one that is in an earlier stage of development.

In short, *never* sell simply to take a profit. You will thereby become over-anxious and chances are you will leap into another commitment without proper analysis and wind up taking a loss that will more than wipe out the previous profit. Stocks should be purchased with intention of holding them forever—or until the time arrives when the UPB has exerted its maximum impact on the rising profit trend.

There is another old slogan that is more confusing than deceiving: "A bull makes money, a bear makes money, but a hog never makes anything." Presumably this is a variation on the "you will never go broke taking a profit" school of thought. However, several interpretations might be applied: (1) this is a soothing bit of rationalization to anyone who sells and watches his stock go up, or buys and watches it go down (2) it's a warning that you will never be able to get the top tick when you sell or the bottom tick when you buy so what's the use of trying? And certainly this is true. (3) It's a jingle thought up by an ingenious customer's man which will work in the subconscious of customers who become seized by inertia and fail to step in and out of the market with desired briskness. In a moment of candor, a broker who is a 30 year veteran in Wall

Street once said: "We don't care *what* they (the customers) do, as long as they do *something*."

A more recent candidate for market maxim immortality: "Anytime is a good time to buy a good stock." Obviously this is 100% true if a "good stock is by definition one that is about to go up. If the requirements of a "good" stock are: (1) rising earnings, a large percentage of which are reinvested in the business, (2) sales rising in good times *and bad* at a rate faster than that of industry as a whole and (3) operating in an industry with above average growth potential, then this maxim is right most of the time. Nevertheless, it should be qualified as follows: "Anytime is a good time to buy a good stock as long as a majority of investors are still in the dark about how good it really is." Much more on this subject in due course.

"Never argue with the tape" would be a truly useful maxim if it was revised to, "never watch the tape." Here again it is not entirely clear just what the original saying means but presumably, it means the same thing as "Never buck the trend." But won't the tape also be wrong at times? Let's assume a stock has moved through 30, 40 and then 50. The tape says the trend is up and you don't argue with the tape. But what if 51 is the final top?

This brings up the pseudo science of "tape reading" as a method of trading. Tape reading should appeal to a person who wants to get something for nothing. The idea is that by watching the price and volume of transactions in a stock as they occur, you will be able to predict whether the stock will rise or decline. The pure tape reader depends on *nothing* but his interpretation of current transactions when making his decisions. This can be a lot of fun—if you don't mind losing your money. The fact is, the tape reader like any other trader is playing a losing game. Watching the tape promotes hasty decisions and in and out trading. Customers would benefit if brokers did away with the tape entirely.

However, there is one important advantage to tape reading we have not yet mentioned. The tape reader must be present at a board room to carry on his mysterious calling. It follows that he won't be under foot at home which clearly promotes better marital relations.

Now for an examination of more specific shortcuts to wealth in the stock market. One of the more enticing routes is via gadgets or charts which reveal what "they" are doing. This, of course, helps you make intelligent decisions about a stock without knowing anything at all about the company's prospects.

CHAPTER 3

Illusions Charted

Certainly, a chart showing the daily price range and volume of U. S. Steel is real enough, as is a chart of the Dow-Jones Average. Or a 200 day "moving" average of that average. Yes, these are real enough, but the interpretation of their future significance is mostly pure illusion.

If time is measured in money then probably the national debt has been surpassed several times over in man hours wasted in an effort to "beat the market" via gadgets of one sort or another.

20 years ago, for example, the writer maintained 400 stock charts on a daily basis, plus numerous "technical market analysis measurements" or gadgets which were supposed to reveal when the market was going up-or down. Or when to buy a stock—or sell it. These playthings wasted about four hours a day which made it necessary to work a 12 hour day to earn a living instead of the usual eight hours.

We had the additional benefit of studying many gadgets developed by subscribers to our advisory service which had a large international circulation. This was a remarkably illuminating experience. Some were even printed on transparent paper. In a bull market you looked from front to back, in a bear market from back to front. A surprisingly large number of individuals were ready and more than willing to show us how we could improve the accuracy of our recommendations. They had a point here since our recommendations were printed in black and white every week and there plainly was much room for improvement. Surprisingly enough, quite a few of these enterprising persons couldn't test their gadgets themselves because they hadn't the funds. Usually they had lost their capital while testing the gadgets that preceded the one that finally worked.

Other and apparently more valuable gadgets were only available at a price. Therefore, we never had the pleasure of studying them. Here is a quote from a typical letter. In other respects the gentleman who wrote this letter was a knowledgeable and rational individual.

After discussing in some detail how inventory control is accomplished by merchants he goes ahead to say:

"I therefore, designed a variable constant (!) that was characteristic of a falling market and the direct reverse which would be characteristic of an advancing market. This was then smoothed out by a moving average and weighted and the obvious action taken as indicated. In other words, I produced a method of following the market with each change in "speed-weight direction" which is exactly what the modern merchant did, instead of arguing with the law of supply and demand and attempting to inject my ideas of value or worth into the picture."

"I honestly feel it would be a good and intelligent buy for you even if used with but one side of the market. It could be of enormous value to the portfolio of an insurance company or endowment fund or pension fund. Since the action takes place only at the opening, I suppose the two of us could operate it, with the provision that we use only our own monies and grow as we will. So, in order to lift myself to a higher and faster scale of operation, I'll sell it for $75,000 and a 4% royalty provided I have permission to use it."

The key sentence in this enlightening letter is the one in which the gadgeteer explains that the gadget does his thinking for him. Come to think of it, this particular gadget may have had some merit after all—for our correspondent it took the place of addiction to more dangerous drugs. But we reluctantly refused to pay $75,000 for the unique way of measuring "speed-weight direction".

Another subscriber had discovered the way to automatically make a fortune in Wall Street. This man was a highly successful business man who after retirement turned to the stock market. He, too, was normal and intelligent in other respects. He had perfected a power line (not to be confused with electrical or telephone lines) which operated in the following manner: "So here is all you do to make this thing work. When the line goes above 15 buy at the next buy spot and hold while the line is above zero. After the line has gone through zero and then makes a lower top, sell it."

"You only need to learn to read the charts for buy and sell spots for if you will hold the chart bottom up and look through the back, the sell short and cover signals will look the same as the buy and sell signals from the front. Therefore, all charts are made on tracing paper."

"I am depending on you to keep this strictly confidential."

In reply to our friendly but somewhat skeptical letter, he stated in part:

"I wrote you originally because your stock selections were not up to par in my opinion and knowing that the power lines would help you materially, I butted in. In your note you mention that it may not work the same way all the time. You forget that I ran the New York Times averages 30 years and snowballed $1000 to over $70 million. That test was done in 1961 and took over a month to do but I think it proved the line."

P.S. "Don't forget to hold the charts bottom up and look through the back for short sales."

Think—this man owned and managed a successful manufacturing corporation before turning his talents to the stock market. The simple fact is, that he and everyone who has evolved a gadget or mechanical system to beat the market are unconsciously deceiving themselves. The illusion here is caused by testing the system on *past* market action.

There are two reasons why this produces misleading results. In the first place, the system will be designed to cope with past conditions which may never again be the same in the future. Now any outside series of happenings can be made to fit and apparently forecast stock market fluctuations. The outcome of football games has been demonstrated as a means of forecasting past bull and bear markets with 100% perfect results. By pure coincidence one team will have won in the past before bull markets commenced, another team before the onset of bear markets. Hence, the reasoning goes one step further, confusing cause and effect, and we have another new gadget for predicting the stock market.

No mechanical system for beating the market has any sounder basis for success than the football score system just cited. Except by pure coincidence no gadget can be right more than 50% of the time. The simple fact is that the future course of the stock market will be determined by events completely unknown to us today. All persons working on new gadgets may quite as well turn to astrology and save themselves a lot of work. There are numerous systems already worked out that use an astrological crystal ball.

But the fanatical chartist will vehemently deny this. Some will even maintain that *any* knowledge about a stock other than past price and volume is a positive disadvantage. In fact, one well-known advisor to the public is said to lock himself up in a windowless room where there is no danger of clouding his crystal ball with fresh air.

Among the most dedicated apostles of technical market analysis are the chartists who search for recurring formations, such as head and shoulders tops (or bottoms), flags, ascending triangles etc. In a nutshell, the theory is that the price-volume action reveals the future trend of the stock. All other information must be cleared from the mind. When mistakes are made it's their faulty interpretation by the chart reader—the chart itself is never wrong. The chart pattern was clearly bullish (or bearish) as the case may be, but the chart reader simply couldn't believe his own chart and hence took no action or what proved to be the wrong action.

Entire books have even been published dealing with this esoteric field of knowledge. As you examine the illustrations and formations you become hypnotized by the perfect sequence of cause and effect. Cynics might go so far as to suspect that the illustrations had been deliberately selected for maximum impact. But more likely the authors have been hypnotized by the illusions created by hindsight.

The flaw in depending on chart formations can be uncovered by using a bit of common sense. Stocks constantly fluctuate in price. Hence, they are always tracing some sort of pattern on a chart. Every top or bottom must reveal a price formation something like a head and shoulders. At times, to see the formation may require considerable imagination on the part of the chartist but there is no such thing as chartists who are lacking in imagination when it comes to patterns. The trouble is that for every head and shoulders top from which a sizable decline does materialize, there will be two or three on the way up from which a decline *doesn't* materialize. The same is true for all other formations. The fact is, the pure chartist will come up with the wrong diagnosis more than 50% of the time. If you doubt this start your own charts and see for yourself.

Frankly, about the only chartists who have remained chartists for very long are those who sell their advice to others. You may ask—How can they retain their clients if they are wrong more often than right? The answer to this can be traced to the gullibility of those individuals who hope to coin a fast dollar and who have failed to do so by their own devices.

Ordinary price charts are created by drawing a vertical line for each day's trading range with a short horizontal line to indicate the closing price. Volume of trading is shown at the bottom of the chart by another vertical line although many technicians like to complicate the situation by adding still another wavy horizontal line which enlightens one as to the average volume over a given period of time.

There is another dedicated group of technicians who are not content with this somewhat primitive chart drawing. So they have developed what they refer to as the "point and figure" technique of charting. Volume is ignored and only price *changes* are recorded. Usually by means of a cross in the appropriate square of the chart paper. The price change may cover one, one-half, two or three points depending on the volatility of the stock. In the case of a one-point chart, if the stock advances nine points before declining one point, nine checks will be entered each one square above the previous one. If the stock then declines, the required number of check marks will be entered each below the last in the next column of squares to the right.

This system is said to have two advantages. The first is that it requires considerably less time and effort which is true and which means the point and figure adherents are on the right track if they waste less time on this activity. The second is that you can not only predict in which direction a stock will move but also *how far* the price will advance or decline.

According to an article in Fortune Magazine, one widely followed point and figure advisor claims traders should realize "a ten percent profit eighty-five percent of the time." Fortune goes on to say:

"To test the claim, Fortune examined every buy and sell signal given on every one of the more than 700 New York Stock Exchange stocks that this advisor routinely covers. The time period covered was the first nine months of 1961; this period was selected instead of the full year because many of the signals given in the last quarter of 1961 were not resolved when this article was being written—i.e., the signals had neither led to a 10 per cent profit (at which point a sale was assumed) nor touched off a stop order. Ninety per cent of the signals given in the nine-month period were resolved.

For the nine months, advisor X's record may be called disappointing, to say the least. Of the stocks tested, nearly 300 gave no signal at all. The remaining stocks gave a total of 855 signals. A trader who acted on these signals would have his 10 per cent profit on 342 trades, or 40 per cent of the time. He would have touched off a stop-loss 426 times (50 per cent), and the average loss would have been 9.98 per cent—i.e., virtually the same as the average profit. One stock, Carter Products, gave (Advisor X) fans an especially hard time: it gave off four buy signals and four sell signals; all but one were losers."

"On the whole, however, they did better on buy signals than on sell signals, perhaps because it was in a rising market. Of the 421 buy recommendations, 220 (52 per cent) made the 10 per cent profit and 180 (43 per cent) were stopped out; of the 434 sell recommendations, only 122 (28 per cent) were profitable, and 246 (57 per cent) were stopped out."

The most serious drawback to buying stocks on the basis of chart action alone is a psychological one. The all-important element of confidence is lacking and this is an essential ingredient of investment success. The investor who owns valid UPB stocks has the faith that is lacking in the technical approach to stock selection. He is much less likely to be "shaken-out" by the endless and meaningless market fluctuations that prove so upsetting to market technicians and all investors who are preoccupied with price fluctuations rather than investment values.

So beware of anyone who has devised a gadget for automatically making money in stocks (or for that matter in anything). He is one of two things—a charlatan or an amateur speculator. After all, the idea that it is possible to, so to speak, push a button then sit back and have the market pay off like a machine is pure illusion. Such systems may work for awhile, then conditions change and the day of reckoning arrives.

In short, the technical approaches are used to rationalize and confirm conclusions arrived at by other—largely intuitive—means. The truth is, all such methods of second guessing the stock market are largely window dressing. Market technicians begin to make money for the first time when they depend less on their charts and more on a sound analysis of future values. The technical approach appears to simplify a complex problem and it does: it badly oversimplifies it. The UPB approach to making long-term profits is also simple in principle, but it requires much more patience and intestinal fortitude and hence, seems unattractive to those who expect to make an easy killing or even just a few fast dollars in the stock market.

CHAPTER 4

Trading Away Your Wealth

The temptation to trade in and out of stocks seems all but irresistible to the person who loses touch with reality when it comes to the stock market. Few "investors" are willing to admit it but even the most conservative of them will, from time to time, jump at the chance to turn a fast dollar.

A personal observation: While in the brokerage business, the writer did an article for Barron's pointing out why it was impossible to trade in and out of stocks and make a profit. (Part of the material in this chapter has been taken from that article). I called the article to the attention of all of my clients who had the urge to trade. Fortunately, for my income, few of them paid any attention to it. They either thought I was wrong or that *they* would be the exception to the rule. In any event, it served a useful purpose. It eased my conscience to some extent to know that I had warned them before we started wheeling and dealing.

Of course, everyone likes to make a few thousand dollars in a few weeks—some prominent market experts even propose that this is the only safe way to make money. This is pure illusion. For the past 20 years I have systematically asked my friends in the brokerage business for the names of people they knew from *first hand obser-vation of their accounts* who had consistently made money over the years trading in stocks. By this I mean profiting on the short swings both in rising and declining markets. To qualify the trader had to be ahead of the game at the end of ten years. *So far I haven't obtained a single name.* Therefore, I can only agree with Bernard Baruch who said that in his lifetime he had only known one successful amateur speculator.

I have known many persons who *said* they had made a lot of money trading, who delighted in recounting their successful trades. But when it came to *documenting* their trading profits it was another story. And there is good reason for this scarcity of successful traders because the mathematical odds are heavily against those seeking short-term profits.

The temptation to trade can be blamed on the infallibil-ity of hindsight. In the stock market as in no other place everything you do is immediately subject to the test of hindsight and the issue is never in doubt. Now plainly the odds are heavily against ever buying a stock without having it sell still lower, or selling without watching it climbing a point or ten points higher. Hindsight always implies that you have made a mistake and worse still that in the future you should actually profit by these "mis-takes."

Consider the mental processes of an investor who bought AT&T some years ago on the theory that conver-sation represented a growth industry and that this growth potential had not yet been adequately discounted by the price of the stock. So he bought some Telephone at 63. It promptly declined to 58, rallied to 62, declined to 55, rallied to 60, declined to 53 and then climbed to 63. Three years had elapsed and Telephone was right back where it was when originally purchased.

After each intermediate top the natural tendency is to say: "I should have sold out and bought back on the next reaction." Only those with the utmost courage can hold a stock that declines from 30 to 20 without resolving that next time he will try to be one of the fortunate few who sells out at 30.

Yet in the end you can't do it. The real trouble is this: When Telephone begins to rally the last time from 53 you say to yourself, when it gets back to the old high of 63 I'll sell out and then re-enter lower down. So finally it does rally to 63 and you sell out only to watch it continue to rise, with the usual reactions, to 150 in 1964 when it was split two for one. The correct procedure in this case as in all cases is to patiently hold on to a stock until the reasons you purchased it in the first place no longer are valid. Never try to "scalp" a few points.

Or, consider the hypothetical case of a trader who accepts two one point profits for every loss of one point in a stock selling at $50.00 per share (no par value). After 45 transactions he has amassed a *gross* profit of $1500, but his cost of doing business amounts to $4050. Hence, if he starts with $5,000 his original capital will be halfed even though his profitable trades have outnumbered his unprofitable ones by a two to one margin.

Let's examine a typical account of a small but active trader following a year when the market had risen without interruption. He wound up the year with a net profit of $2500. Incidentally, if he had done nothing all year but hold the stocks he started with, his paper profits would have exceeded $5,000. His commissions plus Federal and State transfer taxes totaled another $3,000. This means the traders *gross* profit amounted to $5500.

Now over a complete market cycle *gross* profits—both realized and unrealized—of everyone who buys and sells securities must approximate gross losses. Therefore, on the loss side of this equation there must be an offsetting $5500 plus an indeterminate amount of expenses. For the sake of this illustration assume such costs of doing business also came to $3000 (actually, this might be more or less depending on the activity in other accounts). Then the total net profit of $2500 must be balanced against someone elses losses of $5500 plus $3000 plus $3000 or $11,500. In this case the mathematical odds are between four and five to one against any one trader garnering a net profit. And this does not allow for the huge profits realized by long-term investors. Moreover, among those who do try for trading profits, a minority of professionals will be the ones who make money at the expense of the host of amateurs who try it. Therefore, the *mathematical* odds are probably more in the order of 10 to 1 against consistently realizing trading profits: The *practical* odds: 100 to 1.

Or, look at it another way. On a typical reaction and rally in an actively traded stock the shares reacted from 46 to 39½, then rallied to 44¾. 550,000 shares changed hands which means brokerage fees and transfer taxes were levied on 11,000 separate transactions. Cost of effecting these trades amounted to about $500,000.

If we assume a trader in this stock is content with a 10% gross profit on each trade, then on this cycle he must buy and sell within one point of the top and bottom of the intermediate swings. Between 39½ and 40½ about 40,000 shares changed hands, between 43¾ and 44¾ about 45,000 shares were traded. Thus, the maximum number who can profit on this particular rally (without selling short) is limited to 40,000 shares out of 550,000 or less than 8%.

If anything these odds are understated by a good deal since they fail to make allowance for one of the biggest stumbling blocks to successful trading—the mechanics of executing orders. The odds here are stacked against even the most nimble operator. To initiate a trade it is almost always necessary to enter orders "at the market". For example, if the bid price for a stock is 35, offered at 35¾, the trader who wants a position in the stock must pay 35¾, not 35. Similarly, when he wishes to sell, if the price at which profits will be taken has been set at 40, and an open sell order entered, the stock may only reach 39½, then turn down. If the bid is subsequently 38, offered at 38¾, the trader who wants to close out his position must do so at 38. In short, if the upswing in question carried from 35 to 39½ the trader who correctly estimated the extent of the move (which is highly unlikely) may only net 2¼ points out of a possible 4½ and this *before* expenses.

If 99% of amateur traders fail, who are the one per cent who succeed? Those who are no longer amateurs: Such as members of the various stock exchanges who enjoy reduced commission rates. But even among these men who make trading a full time job only the most astute survive. And even these professionals might do much better in the long run if they devoted an equal amount of work to selecting UNIQUE PROFIT BREAKTHROUGH stocks and then held them indefinitely.

Always remember: Those investors who hold for long-term gains over a period of years must profit to the extent that amateur traders who try for quick profits lose.

In the old days a speculator was not stymied by high income taxes on short-term security profits. This one disadvantage alone makes profitable trading a thing of the past. The tax laws are stacked against the trader and it's well for the person who embarks upon the rocky trading road to consider the mathematics of paying taxes on the big killing he dreams about.

We talked recently with a man who had quit a good job a few months ago to devote full time to short-term trading. He was operating with $100,000 and estimated he could make $35,000 a year although he had been following the market for less than a year. We mentioned the tax angle and he said he viewed the tax just as though he was paying it on a salary.

But there is quite a bit of difference between a fixed salary and short-term profits in the market. Because even the most astute trader will suffer losses along with the profits. Let us assume our optimistic friend made almost twice as much as he lost (the reverse is a much more probable outcome). In short, he does wind up with profits of $35,000 this year and loses only $20,000 next year. If he has no other source of income he will be in the 50% bracket and so will pay the government $17,500. If his living expenses are $10,000 a year, at the end of the first year his capital has increased to $107,500. At the end of the second year and a $20,000 loss, although he is still ahead $15,000 on paper, his capital will have *decreased* to $87,500. The difference can only be recouped out of future profits. But these profits will be harder to come by since he is operating with less capital.

Some prominent advisors advocate placing, "all your eggs in one basket and then watching the basket". And who doesn't watch a stock like Syntex skyrocket from 20 to 190 in a few months and think how nice it would be to have all of his money in it? It would be gratifying, but don't, under any circumstances, try it. In any year, such moves occur in only a handful of the several thousand actively traded stocks.

The odds are prohibitive against selecting such a stock and then managing to buy near the bottom and sell near the top. Meanwhile, there is a very real danger of getting into a commitment when everything looks bright, only to have some unexpected reverse send the stock plummeting. Such an experience can be demoralizing as well as costly. The "all or nothing" trader violates every principle of successful investing and is certain to fail, and fail spectacularly in the long run. However, a good case can be made for limited diversification and "watching the basket" in investment accounts that are supervised continuously.

The hazards of speculating are as old as mankind. Even before the days when a sizable slice of profits was confiscated by the state, the individual who attempted to make a fast dollar seldom succeeded. The ancients were fully aware of the dangers involved although their opportunities for investment were more limited than ours. The richest man in the fabled city of Babylon complied *Five Laws of Gold* which have been passed down to posterity.

The fifth law warned; "Fanciful propositions that thrill like adventure tales always come to the new owner of gold. These appear to endow his treasure with magic powers that will enable it to make impossible earnings. Yet heed ye the wise men for verily they know the risks that lurk behind every plan to make great wealth suddenly."

This piece of advice is quite as sound in the year 1965 A.D. as in 1965 B.C.

Even with a crystal ball you couldn't trade successfully. The trader would lose in the end even if he knew in advance what the market was going to do. If he knew an intermediate top would occur in January, a bottom in April, another top in July, and another bottom in October (incidentally, this is a fairly sound forecast most any year), the problem of selecting stocks that would conform to this pattern and paying expenses would still preclude making money consistently.

If you have a yen to make a fast dollar switch from Wall Street to Nevada where the odds are much more favorable. We have seen that the odds in the stock market are in the order of at least 10 or 100 to 1 against a trader. In a casino the odds are close to even up or 50–50 in all games except the slot machines and roulette. In roulette the house percentage is an exact 5.6%. In craps the mathematical advantage is only about 1.5%. The odds are more difficult to figure on 21—the most popular casino game. However, extensive calculations and tests reveal that the dealers advantage is somewhere between ½ of 1% and 1%. The actual house take may run up to 4% or 5% because the average player seldom knows the correct plays to make. If you want to gamble, odds of

51 to 49 against you look a lot more attractive than 100 to 1 or even 10 to 1. As a matter of fact, the house percentage in a game like 21 is less than the commission charged to buy or sell 100 shares of stock on the New York Stock Exchange.

The foregoing should not be construed as an endorsement of gambling. Here too, you lose in the end, but meanwhile you have a fighting chance—at least you get a run for your money. Also, it has been rumored that many gamblers don't pay income taxes on their winnings (as they should). This might be termed an intangible tax shelter comparable in importance to the tax exempt features of municipal bonds.

Here is a parting thought: Most of the famous speculators died broke or as suicides. Even before the days of high income taxes and taxes on capital gains, successful traders were few and far between. Those who made and kept fortunes—men like Bernard Baruch—a legend in his own day—and William Durant, always thoroughly investigated a company and the industry before investing. They hired engineers and other experts to prepare detailed reports on its operations and potential resources. If, in their own judgment, the future value was substantially greater than the current market prices, if there was a UPB possibility, they took a position and then patiently waited for the underlying value to be fully reflected in price.

As anyone who follows stock prices knows, they can go down with frightening rapidity. A rise that took six months can be wiped out in six days. This leads to the illusion that it is easy to make money selling short. As we shall see in reality it is anything but easy.

CHAPTER 5

Don't Sell America Short

Such was the sage advice of J. P. Morgan. It is also the policy of most of the nation's brokerage firms. They usually have two rules concerning how employees (and very often the partners themselves) may invest their own personal funds. Rule 1: No short selling is permitted, and Rule 2: Stocks may not be purchased on margin.

These rules contain the distilled wisdom of some of the shrewdest brains on Wall Street. At first glance one might conclude: "If a broker who devotes his entire time to the stock market shouldn't sell short, who should? There is a simple answer to this question. *"No one* who wants to make money in the stock market should sell short."

Making money on the short side of the market is more difficult than making money on the long side. In the first place, for tax purposes *all* short sales are considered to be short-term transactions *regardless* of how long the position is actually held. Short sellers are traders par excellent and subject to all the disadvantages discussed in the previous chapter, plus a number of others peculiar to short selling alone.

Theoretically, it should be possible to garner more rapid profits by selling short than by buying stocks for a rise, because stocks often retrace in a few days a rise of several months duration. This, however, is pure illusion. Theoretically, you can count every grain of sand in the Sahara Desert. In practice it can't be done. The same is true of short selling. The very fact that timing must be much more accurate when selling short than when buying to hold makes it impractical.

Also, it is often impossible to sell short at the desired price. Since the Security Act of 1934, short sales can only be filled after all long sales at that price have been executed and only on an "uptick". That is, a stock can be sold short only at a price higher than the previous different price. This rule was enacted to prevent the price of a stock being artifically depressed by old-time "bear raids" during periods of market weakness.

Still another disadvantage: In addition to the usual attrition of brokerage commissions plus State and Federal transfer taxes, the short seller must pay dividends, when declared, to the person from whom the stock was borrowed. Moreover, there is the ever-present danger that the stock borrowed will be called by the lender. If the broker is unable to borrow the stock elsewhere, the short seller is forced to cover whether he wants to or not. Although this rarely happens, when it does, it is usually at the worst possible time for the short seller, *i.e.,* when prices are rising steadily and the floating supply (stock in the hands of brokers and therefore, eligible for lending) is diminishing. At such times it may be necessary to pay a premium to borrow the stock which further adds to the expense of selling short.

The bear must also buck the *long-term* trend of stock prices which has always been UP. Only once or twice in each generation does a bear market occur comparable in magnitude to the several intervening bull markets, a fact which prompted J. P. Morgan to utter his famous piece of advice. Even during times when the market is moving sidewise, stocks advance two days for each day they decline. An investor who owns a stock can, if his financial condition permits, hold it forever. He is under no obligation to sell. Not so the short seller. Sooner or later, he *must* cover the stock and return it to the owner. This fact was immortalized by the famous bear, Daniel Drew, in a couplet, the meaning of which is more accurate than the grammar:

"He who sells what isn't his'n
"Must buy it back or go to prison."

And the last, but by no means the least, drawback to selling short is the insecure psychological attitude of the speculator who sells short and then watches his stock begin to climb. The speculator who buys a stock knows the worst that can happen is for it to decline to zero. But, for the short seller there is no limit to how high a stock can rise. Looking at the other side of the equation, it is mathematically impossible for the short seller to realize a gain of more than 100% on his capital, and in practice the ultimate falls far short of this. But the owner of a stock may watch his investment increase in value 100, 500 or even 1,000%, and there are millions of investors who have realized such gains over the years. And many more will do so in the future if they follow the rules in this book.

Probably the most famous short selling debacle of all time occurred in 1901 as a result of the fight between Harriman and Morgan for control of the Northern Pacific

Railroad. Both sides bought and locked up all the stock offered between 90 and 180. Speculators who had no way of knowing what was happening sold short heavily all the way up. As the stock continued to rise, investors, who had loaned stocks to speculators for short selling, called in their stock to sell at the unbelievably high prices. When it became clear that the stock was cornered, *i.e.,* that more shares had been sold short than could be bought back, short sellers frantically bought at any price. On May 9, 1901 Northern Pacific actually sold at $1,000 a share and other market leaders declined 30, 40 or 50 points as speculators sold them at any price to raise funds to buy in their Northern Pacific shorts. When the extent of the panic became evident, the Morgan-Harriman interests agreed to permit all the short sellers to buy in their stock at a set price of $150 per share. Admittedly, this is an exceptional case, but, even in the ordinary course of business similar catastrophies—though on a smaller scale—constantly plague those who try to profit on the short side of the market.

It is, therefore, little wonder that few fortunes have been taken out of Wall Street via the short selling route. A majority of the old-time professionals who favored the short side of the market are said to have died broke. Even during the Golden Days (for short selling) from 1929 to 1932, for every speculator who cleaned up on the short side there were hundreds who were cleaned out on the way up. And those who did sell short near the top covered their short positions far too soon, went long on margin and were wiped out by repeated waves of forced and panic induced selling.

The record of the amateur short seller as revealed by

the trading in odd lots must be even more dismal, since these individuals invariably sell heavily at every market bottom. And on no occasion since these statistics became available in 1939 have they sold short to any extent at or near market tops. Total short interest on the New York Stock Exchange follows a similar though less reliable pattern. Short interest as a percentage of total trading shows a marked tendency to reach peak levels at important bottoms and to diminish near important tops.

Short selling has always been criticized by social reformers, largely on the ground that it artificially depresses the price of stocks and causes losses, (either paper or real) to true investors. The inference is that short sellers profit at the expense of investors. The facts suggest that by definition the reverse must be closer to the truth. If the bears do profit, they must supply stocks when prices are high and support stocks when prices are low, which presumably would help prevent abnormally large price swings. Actually, all available evidence suggests that investors profit at the expense of short sellers—a situation which social reformers presumably will not find fault with.

One thing is certain; speculators who strive for quick profits, and therefore, those who engage in short selling, improve the market's liquidity, thereby enabling investors to buy or sell to better advantage. It is a matter of common observation that large blocks can be bought or sold with very little price concession in stocks that are speculative favorites and in which a large short interest exists. On the other hand, it may require a several point concession in price to dispose of a large block of stock which lacks an active speculative following.

One important reason today's markets are very thin is

because of the decline of the speculator (and short seller). This is clearly evident if we assume the amount of short selling is a rough gauge of overall speculative activity. In recent years, the short interest on the New York Stock Exchange has averaged around five million shares, a goodly portion of which was represented by "arbitrage" operations and selling "against the box." In contrast, before the income tax reduced the attractiveness of short-term gains, short interest regularly exceeded this figure, and this at a time when about one-tenth as many shares were listed on the New York Stock Exchange. Expressed in terms of per cent of average volume of trading, short interest in recent years has averaged about 1%. This figure has exceeded 2% only twice since 1932 and for only a few weeks each time. Reliable data on the amount of short selling before 1931 are not available, but it must have averaged well above 2%. At one time in 1931, short selling accounted for more than 4% of total volume of trading.

Today's short interest in individual stocks is hardly worth mentioning in comparison with what was common during the early Thirties. Thus, the short interest in U. S. Steel recently amounted to 17,003 shares out of the 54,136,437 shares listed. In General Motors 30,683 shares were short out of 287,180,318 shares listed. In comparison, on June 1, 1932—near the bottom of the 1929–1932 bear market—the short interest in U. S. Steel was no less than 453,486 shares out of 8,703,000 listed. In General Motors, 486,232 shares were sold short out of 43,500,000 listed. In that speculative era, it was not unheard of for the number of shares sold short in one stock to exceed 50% of the total outstanding. To cite an example, on August 28, 1931, the short interest in J. I. Case reached the unbelievable total of 139,000 shares or 71% of the 195,000 shares outstanding.

In a nutshell then, the hazards of short selling are not confined to being caught in a cornered market such as plagued the shorts in Northern Pacific. Rather the hazards stem from a multitude of small disadvantages which sooner or later trip up all but the most seasoned professional trader who pays a reduced commission rate. It is fortunate, indeed, that the intricacies of selling short discourage the vast majority of speculators from taking the plunge, because the published statistics on short selling suggest the odds are overwhelmingly against anyone who is bearish on the stock market and has the temerity to back his opinion with cash.

Here a word about short selling "against the box" may be in order. It is often cited as a useful way of protecting paper profits after stock prices have risen to dangerous levels. Actually, in recent years since the loophole in the tax laws was closed which permitted investors to translate short-term profits into long-term capital gains by selling short, the advantages of short selling "against the box" seem largely illusionary.

Thus, assume an investor decides to sell short a stock in which he has a large paper profit; the stock subsequently declines substantially and he covers at a large profit. The profit on the short sale is short-term and taxed at the maximum rate (in fact, his tax may actually be increased if the short-term profit boosts him into a higher bracket). Meanwhile, he has watched an equal paper profit disappear which could have been realized and taxed at the lower capital gains rate. It would seem then that the sensible course would simply be to establish at least part of the paper profit in the first place and pay the capital gains tax on it. In this way double commission expense can also be avoided.

In the market as elsewhere, the road to failure is paved with the best of intentions. So it is with those who, as we have seen, hope to preserve their capital by holding 100% cash during periods of uncertainty (which is about 99% of the time) or even with those who wish to play it safe by investing for income. Here again we have the moral contrast of fear vs. courage.

CHAPTER 6

The Income Illusion

One of the most fundamental mistakes an investor can make is to buy stocks for income. Yet this seems to be the normal stock selection yardstick employed by many investors who haven't made a study of correct investment principles. If a stock yields 7% it looks like a better buy than a stock that yields 6% which, in turn, looks better than a stock yielding 5%. And so on down the scale. Now actually the reverse reasoning is much more likely to be true. The stocks with the best future seldom appear cheap in relation to other stocks although there are exceptions, as we will see. They invariably will return less than stocks with mediocre or poor appreciation potential.

Investors who require income to meet living expenses should invest in exactly the same stocks that investors seeking capital growth select. If necessary, current income requirements should be met by withdrawals from capital. In due time, the UPB stock that yields a paltry 2% today, will yield more—based on today's cost—than the stock that currently returns 6 or 7%.

What if you had been attracted by the 10% yield on South Puerto Rico Sugar in 1964? It was a danger signal. Following the dividend cut in 1965 and despite the fact that the stock declined some 15 points, the return declined to only 2%.

In contrast, 15 years ago Minnesota Mining and Manufacturing returned a niggardly 2%, but today investors who bought the stock at that time enjoy a generous annual return of 20% on their *original* investment. Meanwhile, MMM still yields less than 2% based on its current price.

In general, the stocks which paid the smallest cash dividends 10 years ago have appreciated more and return more today than those issues which were being purchased 10 years ago for their liberal return. There is little doubt that in this one respect, at least, history will repeat itself during the next ten or twenty years. If you have the choice of buying a stock that yields 2% or one yielding 7% and have no other information at all about the two stocks you should, without hesitation, select the low yielding issue. You can bet that it will turn out to be the better investment of the two.

Better still, buy a stock that pays no dividend whatsoever (provided it qualifies under the Unique Profit Breakthrough rules blueprinted in a subsequent chapter). Thus, if a growth company can realize 10, 20, or even 30% on reinvested earnings why should they pay these earnings to shareholders who must then pay a second income tax on them?

The stone age belief that a high dividend rate denotes a good investment dies slowly. Witness the fact that a stock usually rises when the dividend is raised, declines when the dividend is cut. Of course, if a modest boost comes in the wake of much larger increase in net income the rise may be warranted. But very often the reverse should occur! For instance, when dividends could be used to better advantage in research activities, plant improvements and so on. Also, bear in mind that many stocks are burdened with a high dividend rate and management is loath to reduce it because they are fearful of an adverse reaction on the part of their stockholders and bankers.

Always remember: The higher the yield, the greater the risk. If the average yield on blue chips is 3%, a good rule would be to *never* buy a stock that yields more than 5% or perhaps 6%. An unusually high yield will be a sure indication that the dividend is about to be reduced (this may be beneficial for the company but not for the owner of the stock). All to often, a stock will be yielding 10%, then the dividend will be cut in half and the yield will soon be 10% again because the shares have fallen 50% in price. Of course, if the standard stocks are yielding 6% to 8% at the bottom of a bear market, stocks yielding from 10% to 12% will be suspect while those returning the liberal 6% to 8% may be perfectly sound values.

Despite the prosperity of the post-war years, there were the usual number of casualties among high yielding stocks. Back in 1951, for example, Celanese returned 7.1% on the $3.00 annual dividend which was an extremely liberal yield for that period. As usual this was a warning that something was wrong. A year later the dividend rate was $2.00 and Celanese still yielded a liberal 7.1%. (Meanwhile, the price has skidded 14 points). By mid-1953, the annual dividend had been reduced to $1.00 and again in 1954, to 50 cents. During those years the stock fell from 46⅝ to below 10. By 1964 earning power had gradually recovered from the low of $.25 a share in 1954 to $4.25 a share. But management wisely adopted a more conservative dividend policy and paid only $1.70 a share to the shareholders in 1964.

Studebaker provides another typical example. Earning power reached a post-war peak in 1950, then trended steadily lower. Yet, by the end of 1953, Studebaker was still paying $3.00 although earnings had fallen below the dividend requirements. At 21, the indicated return was 14.3%. Again this was a clear cut signal to sell or avoid the stock. Shortly thereafter, the dividend was omitted entirely and Studebaker nosedived to around 2½.

More recently, another auto stock—American Motors—was selling at 11 and paying an annual dividend of $1.00 a share for a big 9.1% return. The next step was predictable: the dividend rate was cut in half.

Some years ago New York New Haven $5 convertible preferred was considered to be a fairly good grade investment. At any rate, the stock sold around 60 for a liberal return of 8.3%. Why the large yield? And why was the stock slowly but steadily trending down when the market was rising? The answer came soon. Earnings plummeted and so did the price of New Haven preferred. Subsequently, the dividend on the preferred was omitted entirely. And eventually the road went into receivership. Yet many holders stubbornly held on to the bitter end.

When the stock sank to 30 they reasoned that they couldn't afford to take such a serious loss and would wait until they could "get out even." Actually they couldn't afford *not* to take their losses because today New Haven is bankrupt and the stock has been delisted. Here again one cardinal principal of successful investing is illustrated: Namely—*never* own a stock with declining earning power unless this is definitely a temporary condition and

50   THE INCOME ILLUSION

the prelude to a UPB which the public is not yet aware of.

Widows seem to be especially income conscious and for an understandable reason. Many of them depend entirely on their investments to meet their current living expenses. Quite naturally they prefer not to draw on their capital and therefore, unless their capital is very large, they tend to favor high yielding stocks. Needless to say, this policy, if followed to its logical conclusion, will cause their capital to shrink at a faster rate than they could have spent it. Eventually, their portfolios will consist entirely of stocks in sluggish, retrogressive industries to the exclusion of issues with appreciation possibilities.

Many of these income conscious people never sell a stock unless they can *reinvest the proceeds at a higher rate of return*. Here is another of the innumerable ways to lose your capital by following a procedure that appears to be logical and beneficial yet is really pure illusion.

To repeat: Common stocks should never be bought for the dividend income they may pay. They should be bought only for long-term gains. At the same time many individuals do need a larger income from their investments than they can get with *safety*. There is no safe solution to this problem other than a savings account at your bank.

When we finally isolate and identify the only type of stocks you should own—Unique Profit Breakthrough Stocks—should you buy all you can and borrow to buy more?

CHAPTER 7

Invest Only Your Own Money

Before 1929 the use of margin was conceded to transform the magic road to wealth from a rocky mountain trail into an eight lane freeway. After 1929 the use of margin was generally viewed as a device invented by the devil. More recently as the country began to accept installment financing as a way of life, the antipathy towards buying stocks on margin has mellowed somewhat. At least today there are about 500,000 or so active margin accounts and we can assume that these individuals, at least, favor its use.

At regular intervals the following argument or an approximation of it is advanced by members of the New York Stock Exchange and other interested parties: "The entire business of the nation is transacted on the basis of credit. Homes and other real estate are purchased with anywhere from nothing to 20% down. Automobiles and other durable goods are purchased on almost equally lenient terms. In view of this, why should the purchase, on credit, of sound investment securities be subject to rigid control by the Federal Reserve System? In recent years the required down payment on stocks has never been less than 50% and has been as high as 100%. This represents discrimination."

On the surface this argument sounds persuasive. And the member firms who advance this argument are certainly sincere. After all, their impassioned pleas for easy margin requirements come straight from the heart because interest on debit balances is their most reliable source of profits.

The appeal of margin trading will always be with us. And who is to say it should be abolished? Those who now borrow money from brokers to speculate would simply borrow from someone else who charged even more interest. Speculators say: "If you have a good thing in 100 shares of Dynamic Electronic Missile Corp. for $2,000, you have an even better thing in 200 shares for the same $2,000." This too sounds convincing—but it's a dangerous illusion. No arguments we put down on paper will convince anyone anyway. The only argument that will carry weight is the experience of buying on maximum margin—not once but 20 or 30 times. In the end the 6% you paid on the debit balance will look like a mighty good return on the original capital.

Investors should have the same right to make mistakes as a young couple who buy more cars and television sets than they can afford because it is so easy to buy on the installment plan. But much evidence suggests that those who advocate the purchase of stocks for cash only are correct. In the first place, the analogy between buying a home or an automobile on borrowed money and buying securities is a poor one. People buy homes to live in but stocks are bought on margin in an effort to make a profit. Moreover, money borrowed to acquire goods is paid back in regular monthly installments. Not so in the case of securities. Stocks can be held on full margin indefinitely

—or at least so long as they don't decline in price to a point where the broker lending the money begins to worry about the safety of his money and asks his customer to put up more margin.

Or, more accurately, when the broker *demands* more margin—or else. The stock market is made up of intangibles but a telegram demanding more margin is not one of them. Fortunately, not so many of these are sent out today as there were before the Federal Reserve controls over margin requirements were introduced. When minimum margin requirements are set at 50% your stocks have to decline to a point where the broker's equity represents less than 25% of the market value of the stock, before you get a call to put up more money. However, the exact point at which margin calls are made varies from broker to broker.

Specifically, let's say you buy a stock at 60 on 50% margin. You put up $3,000 and your broker puts up the other $3,000. Now suppose the stock declines to 40. If you sell you realize $1,000 ($4,000 less the $3,000 you borrowed) so your equity is 25% of the market value of the stock. If you don't sell and it goes still lower (these things do happen) you must always put up enough more money to restore the required 25% ratio. You can see by this pleasant little example that when the stock goes down one-third you lose two-thirds of your original investment. This may be rightly construed by some people as a disadvantage.

In general, the maxim "never meet a margin call" is correct but it, too, has its disadvantages. Especially, toward the end of a severe market setback when stocks will often open sharply lower on heavy volume. These sellers are the hapless speculators—on margin—who have failed to make the call and whose stock is being dumped by the broker "at the market". When this selling is out of the way prices naturally rebound with great vigor which effectively adds insult to injury for those who were sold out. How much of a selling climax can be attributed to forced selling in margin accounts?

Precise figures are difficult to obtain, but certainly such selling will not originate from institutions and trusts. And the statistics on odd lot trading clearly indicate that the "public"—to use the term loosely—will invariably be buying heavily rather than selling. Professionals such as specialists and floor traders will generally be on the buying side. Who, then, is selling so urgently? The only conclusion is that individuals whose sound judgment has taken a back seat to emotionally inspired fear must account for the selling. What could logically cause this fear? Overextended positions which is to say, holding stocks on margin.

Additional selling at such times will originate from traders who have entered stop loss orders below the market before the final sell-off. These individuals, of course, get whipsawed and resolve thereafter (correctly) never to use stop orders.

But leaving the hapless customer out of it for a moment—after all he doesn't *have* to use margin—the real case against margin is that it exaggerates price swings which are violent enough without this added stimulus. Bull markets are fueled on credit—let there be no mistake about it. Bear markets are extended by the liquidation of such credit.

Many statistics could be cited to prove this statement

but one series should be enough. Whenever margin requirements are raised the stock market turns down shortly thereafter and vice versa after a reduction. There is no doubt that if stocks were dealt in for cash only the *big* bull and bear markets would be a thing of the past. We would still have gradually rising or declining price trends over the long pull as prices adjusted to changing conditions, but the price of a stock would not change substantially over a short period of time without any change at all in the earnings, dividends and prospects of the company. This, of course, is the usual rather than the exceptional thing today.

Now, admittedly, many people would suffer by the abolition of margin trading. Violent market swings make for good brokerage business. Rapid price changes seem to encourage more frequent action by customers. As a matter of fact, volume of trading always drops when prices are holding in a narrow channel. From long experience, we would guess that at least 75% of transactions on the stock exchanges are completely needless; that the investors making these transactions would have been dollars ahead if they had done nothing at all but hold the stocks they originally owned.

If volume dropped by 75% or if it drops at all for that matter, we are told that the market's liquidity would be severely impaired. Presumably, the greater the number of transactions the better the market for a stock. That is to say, the stock can be either bought or sold with a smaller change from the previous price than would otherwise be the case.

So far as we know this contention has never been challenged, so now is the time to issue one: By and large, the widest price fluctuations occur in the most actively traded stocks. True enough, these active stocks generally have a spread of only ⅛ or ¼ points between the bid and asked prices. But then this is also true of many issues that trade only a few hundred shares a day. Moreover, the year's price range of these stocks is generally much smaller than the range of the active market leaders.

One reason that margin trading tends to exaggerate market swings is because it gradually undermines one's ability to think clearly. It is a fact that broker's loans rise and decline with prices. Individuals trading on margin view their operations differently than does the person who owns his stocks outright. The margin trader is more subject to extremes of emotionally inspired greed and fear.

After the market has risen for a long time the speculator can see that "they" must be coining money as stock after stock shoots up in rotation. Supposedly astute market men will be endorsing the theory of "pyramiding" or averaging up. Owning stocks on margin seems to be the progressive, sensible thing to do. As a result the average speculator will hold his maximum position on full margin when prices are high rather than low.

For awhile this leverage produces magic results—on paper. Then the market starts down and keeps going. Fear begins to replace greed. After awhile the profits disappear and losses begin to grow at a rate twice as great as if the stocks were not held on margin. The speculator can imagine all too vividly what his financial position would be if stocks sink much lower. At last he can't stand the strain and says to himself: "They can have them at any price." So he sells out—or is sold out by a margin call he can't meet—at or near the low. He then either quietly retires from the market or else resolves to buy stocks only for cash—a resolution that lasts until the next big speculative spree when everyone around him seems to be doubling and tripling his money in a matter of weeks.

One concluding remark about using margin as an investment tool to increase income. Tabulations are regularly distributed showing how you can boost your dividend income by buying liberal dividend paying stocks on margin. On paper this may work but it does not work out in practice. For one thing, most of these tabulations ignore the increased costs of buying twice as many shares of stock. For another they entail the use of a speculator's tool to achieve an investors goal without taking into consideration the psychological effect that owning stocks on margin can have on the investor. And finally, such an operation doubles the margin for error since buying stocks primarily for income is bad enough let alone buying them with borrowed money.

So much for the merits of borrowing. Now let us look at a highly sophisticated way to beat the market. A way that is "in" among "smart" operators.

CHAPTER 8

The Trend Followers

One ultra sophisticated solution to investing makes an almost irresistible appeal to all those out to make a killing in the market in a hurry. This is the trend following philosophy and a surprisingly large number of well-known market analysts are disciples. They argue that a fundamental appraisal of a company's relative value or future prospects is a waste of time. Instead, you should act only on the basis of a stock's trend. This school argues that you should wait until an uptrend is established or until a "saucer" or "head and shoulders" bottom has been *completed* before buying. They then wait for the reverse pattern to develop to give them a sell signal. The idea is to concentrate your funds in stocks that are moving up the fastest.

Now to base investment decisions on price action *alone* strikes us as plain silly—about as logical as buying a business today for $100,000 and selling it next week for $80,000, on the theory that since this is the best price available the price trend is down, and therefore, you should sell out.

The theory behind trend following (of which The Dow Theory is the best known example) is that everything that everyone knows about a company is reflected in the price

59

of its stock. Thus, the theory goes, informed professional and insider buying will be revealed on the ticker tape—at least to those skilled in reading the silver screen. When volume expands on the upside, for example, it means the pros are beginning to buy, and vice-versa, when volume expands on down ticks.

This sounds convincing but it simply is not true. *As a general rule, insiders buy on weakness and sell on strength.* Thus, during the rising markets of 1959 and 1961 insiders were heavy sellers, but on the 1960 and 1962 declines they were heavy *buyers.* In short, unusual activity on the tape is rarely informed insider buying or selling. It is more likely to originate from board room sitters, and the public in general, who are always attracted by higher prices and increased activity.

Moreover, professional and insider transactions combined account for no more than 25–30% of total trading. This explains why the public, not the professionals, are chiefly responsible for bull and bear trends in the stock market. And this also explains why chart and trend followers will, in the long run, suffer more losses than profits.

Another favorite ploy of the trend followers is that of buying "on-a-scale-up." This theory dates back to the days of Jesse Livermore, when a few professional speculators (*i.e.,* gamblers) dominated the market. In those days technical market analysis and trend following made more sense because very little fundamental company data and no insider trading information was available to investors. But, we are at a loss to explain why this theory still has followers today—at least among *investors* who should strive to buy the largest possible number of shares for each dollar invested. We are certainly not arguing against paying a higher price for a stock if you are unable to fill your requirements at a lower price. But, we are against the folly of *waiting* for the higher price before buying as the trend followers advocate doing.

The trend follower is motivated by two things. First, he doesn't want to own stocks when the "market" is in a bear trend. And second, he doesn't want to continue to own any stock in his account that has turned down. Now, by definition, these two facts can't be known until *after* they occur. So the speculator is constantly asking himself: Is the current reaction in the stock market the beginning of a new major decline? Is the reaction in my stock the beginning of a major trend reversal? Unfortunately, the answers to these questions are not available until it is too late (from the trader's point of view) to take the action which he can see in retrospect would have produced the desired results. As a result, the trend follower lives in a constant state of frustration because he constantly needs to make decisions (even to do nothing) that must be based on insufficient evidence.

This is not to say that the price action of a stock should be ignored. Often unusual activity will alert you to a development you might otherwise have overlooked. But it is seldom desirable to take action on the basis of price trends *alone* and this is especially true when buying.

Trend following can also be applied to industry groups when one industry after another catches the fancy of speculators. First it will be the airlines, then the drugs, then the golds and so on. The idea here is to bet on the horses that are in the lead, *i.e.*, concentrate in the hot industries. When the drugs cool off, switch to the golds, when the golds slow down, switch to the autos or whatever is on the move.

Figures have been published which show that if you had started with only $100 in 1915 and concentrated in the strongest industry group thereafter, your investment would currently be worth around $100 billion. To illustrate the idea: From 1929 to 1932 when the great bear market was underway you would have held gold stocks. In 1955 you would have held aluminums, in 1959–1960 bowling stocks, etc.

This, of course, is all pure illusion. To even attempt trend following is to court disaster for the same reasons discussed earlier. By the time the individual stock has gained the spotlight it is usually dangerously overvalued or by the time the industry is hot the trend may be about to reverse. In either case, the trend follower must make *daily* decisions: To hold another day or sell? Exercising objective judgment becomes an impossibility under such conditions.

As we shall see this is one reason why the trend following concept breaks down completely when it is applied to the trend of the market as a whole.

CHAPTER 9

Can The Stock Market Forecast?

The Dow Theory represents one offshoot of the trend following school of thought. Briefly it holds that stock prices move with the regularity of the tides. When the tide begins to ebb (that is a series of lower highs and lower lows has been witnessed) you sell stocks. Later on when the tide starts to come in again (a series of higher lows and higher highs) you buy them back.

The lack of reality in such an endeavor has been discussed. But one additional thought: During the long intervals when the market averages—but not individual stocks—are moving sidewise, followers of the Dow Theory suffer one demoralizing whipsaw after another. A more unrealistic, unworkable approach to investing could hardly be devised.

One proposition of the Dow Theory seems especially intriguing. Namely, that the trend of stock prices reflects the combined wisdom of the best minds in the investment world. The idea is that the price of a stock or the trend of the market reflects the rational, considered judgment of those in the best position to know and weigh the thousands of influences affecting the value of securities.

To illustrate, it is only logical to assume that the officers and directors of a corporation are in a position to know more about the company's affairs than anyone else. If the outlook is discouraging presumably they will sell and advise their friends to sell. On the other hand, if everything looks rosy they and others "in the know" will be quietly accumulating the stock.

This is happening all the time and will be discussed later in detail. Knowledge of such activity can be of great help in stock selection. But such knowledgeable transactions, may be overshadowed for long intervals by uninformed buyers and sellers. Probably 90% of the trading in any stock is accounted for by people who have no inside information at all. Most likely they will be buying because other stocks are moving up in a contagious fashion. Or, they will sell because they have a small profit, or are fearful a bear market is underway and so on.

Or what if the sweet little lady down the street inherits a block of stock in a tobacco company and proceeds to sell it because she doesn't believe in smoking? (If this sounds far-fetched, bear in mind that investment counselors seldom recommend liquor or tobacco stocks for this very reason). Clearly, the resulting price decline is about as significant as the conjunction of Venus and Jupiter in so far as the future of the company is concerned. Yet, most *short-range* trends are the result of equally irrational behavior on the part of buyers and sellers.

Thirty years ago William Peter Hamilton and Robert Rhea pointed out how the Dow-Theory not only forecasts the trend of stock prices but also constitutes a sensitive barometer of future business activity. When the Dow Theory signaled a bear market the business cycle was about to turn down, when the averages, after a long decline, established a series of higher highs and higher lows, business would improve soon thereafter. There was much to be said for this point of view 30 or 40 years ago but not today.

In fact, today the *lack* of correlation between market trends and business activity is a more dependable barometer. It follows that the stock market is usually *wrong* rather than right about the future of business—if by being right we mean that the market cycle should lead the business cycle by an interval of a few months. (Most commentators assume that business conditions determine stock prices but even this assumption is open to question. Quite a strong case can be made for the opposite assumption: Namely, that the state of the securities markets has a greater effect on business than vice-versa.)

This perverse relationship has only come about in recent years due to government regulation of business, credit and stock market procedures. In earlier days the stock market was a reliable barometer or, more accurately, mirror of business conditions. Not because of the clairvoyance of those buying and selling stocks but because the flow of capital between industry and the stock market followed a recurring pattern. Markets rose with prosperity and declined with adversity.

Today this is all changed. During the post-war years the redistribution of wealth and high taxes have produced a chronic shortage of venture capital. When business is good more working capital as well as capital for expansion is needed. At least this is the time—rightly or wrongly—when most businessmen see fit to expand. But this is precisely the time when loans are hardest to float. Consequently, hundreds of thousands of small businessmen all over the country sell stocks or bonds to raise money to finance their expanding business operations. This selling depresses stock prices.

Then business turns down. Money becomes cheaper, inventories are cut back and cash begins to accumulate. These idle funds quickly find their way into the stock and bond markets. Thus, we have a paradoxical situation: Stocks boom during recessions and turn dormant or decline during the later stages of the periods of greatest business prosperity.

Consider the record. Between 1938 and mid-1943, industrial production staged one of the most spectacular recoveries ever witnessed due, of course, to the war. The usual explanation for the depressed level of stock prices is that investors were fearful that we might lose the war. And even if we won the impact of the excess profits tax on net income would be bearish. A more likely reason was the fact that businessmen were selling stocks to raise money to expand existing businesses or start up new ones. Prices were rising on every side, larger inventories were required, new plants were needed and capital flowed out of the stock market into business channels to accommodate this need. Moreover, British interests were selling American stocks to help finance their war effort.

From 1943 to early 1946 business activity slumped badly. Defense plants had been completed while consumer goods and private building activities were still restricted. As a result, capital lay idle. But not for long. An all inclusive bull market in stocks was getting underway which ended in May 1946 or about the time industrial production began to *pick up*.

The next three years witnessed a period of rapidly expanding sales, earnings and dividends. But strangely enough stock prices continued to slide gradually lower.

The orthodox explanation is that majority opinion was expecting a post-war depression, investor confidence was at a low ebb and therefore people refused to buy stocks. But the truth is that few investors can hold cash for longer than a month or two. Again, the real reason the market was under pressure was because money was once again flowing out of stocks and into capital goods for the formation of new businesses and the expansion of existing ones. Money was going into consumer and durable goods, inventories, new homes and similar uses, rather than into stocks. The stock market was financing the early post-war boom.

But when a recession finally struck in 1949, the stock market again took off and continued straight up until January–February of 1951. The business boom of 1951–1953 once again unfolded against a background of generally lower stock prices and the peak of the boom (August 1953) missed coinciding with the *bottom* in stock prices (September 1953) by only one month. Throughout the recession of 1954 (which had the usual adverse effect on corporate earnings), stocks soared and for the same reasons we have already mentioned. But once again during the business boom of 1955–1957 stocks marked time at first and then declined sharply.

Old timers who acted on the classical procedure of buying stocks when business was depressed and selling during periods of great prosperity must have lost a great deal of money during these years. They learned one thing, at least: The stock market is no longer a reliable barometer of future business conditions. The classical objective of buying at the bottom and selling at the top has become vastly more difficult than in the past.

Does the stock market, then, discount future developments within individual industries and stocks any better? (Technical analysis of market and stock trends becomes a logical impossibility if the answer *is* NO) and the answer is NO, at least 50% of the time. Thus, in 1945 alone the airlines soared 100% on average. As it turned out the market was discounting an imminent *collapse* in earning power which found the industry reporting large deficits in 1947.

Between 1946 and 1949 paper stocks steadily declined while earnings quadrupled. What was the market discounting? As it turned out paper company earnings and dividends continued to expand, albeit more slowly, for another eight years. The paper group then registered its highest price just before earnings turned down. A hundred similar examples could be given.

Far from being a barometer of the future, stocks tend to discount concrete developments *after,* rather than before, they occur. *Intangible* prospects, to be sure, may be discounted months or years in advance. Then when hopes finally become reality the stocks affected proceed to decline.

In summary, the evidence clearly reveals that a ten year old child can forecast the future as well as the stock market can. However, this does not mean that *no one* can look into the economic future with a better than average record. Some people are luckier than others. But, by definition, majority opinion certainly can't.

As we proceed further we encounter more and more convincing solutions to the problem of investing in stocks. Dollar averaging is one that deserves special investigation.

CHAPTER 10

The Golden Egg

A vast amount of literature is published each year depicting the advantages of systematic investment in stocks via dollar averaging. These studies will show how phenomenal appreciation could have been realized by a person who invested $1000 each year since 1900 or 1920 in stocks like General Motors, Dow Chemical, Jersey Standard and the like. All this is perfectly correct. But, as usual, hindsight is involved. In practice, an extremely long period is required for final success and the enormous difference in final results is a function of the vehicle initially selected for investment. Thus, what happened to a person who regularly invested in Arcturus Radio Tube or some long-forgotten manufacturer of electric autos or buggy whips?

Yet, the theory behind dollar averaging is sound enough, chiefly because these plans preclude trying to second guess the market. The person who adopts such a plan knows, *in advance,* exactly what action he will take under every conceivable condition and when he will take it. This alone is a tremendous advantage in mastering the always baffling stock market.

The success of a program actually depends on the *averaging down* part, not on the purchases made at progressively higher prices. Since equal *dollar* amounts of stock are purchased at fixed intervals, fewer shares will be purchased when prices are high, more when prices are low. As a result, the average cost of the shares acquired is always lower than the average of the prices paid.

For such a program to succeed two conditions must be met. (1) A stock must be selected which will fluctuate in price and will also rise in price over a period of time by a margin sufficient to at least offset any decrease in the purchasing power of the dollar and (2) Anyone embarking on a dollar averaging program must be absolutely (not just reasonably) certain that the program can be continued for many years *without interruption*. Success depends on being able to buy more stock when prices are lowest—which is usually at a time when business is bad and unemployment is high. This, of course, is precisely the time when most people are having trouble (which they did not anticipate) even meeting day-to-day living expenses.

Even those individuals who do have ample purchasing power may become discouraged with a program which has netted them nothing but paper losses for a number of years. If the fortunes of the company they are investing in take a turn for the worse they will doubt (correctly) the wisdom of continuing with the program. Consider the investor who systematically invested in Tri-Continental Corp. As the table on page 71 reveals spectacular results were realized in the end. But if because of unforeseen circumstances he was forced to liquidate his position in 1941 or 1942 when Tri sold as low as ⅝, his loss amounted to 50% or more of his original investment. Furthermore, at that time net asset value was less than nothing, which hardly inspired continued confidence in the stock as a vehicle for a conservative dollar averaging program. The table below is reproduced with permission of Barron's. It shows the result of investing $500 each quarter in the Dow Jones Industrial average, General Motors, Woolworth, Tri-Continental (a closed end trust), Mutual Fund "A"—a common stock fund and Mutual Fund "B" a balanced Fund.

DOLLAR AVERAGING SINCE 1939

Year	Capital Invested	Dow-Jones Industrials	General Motors	Woolworth *	Tri-Continental	Mutual ** Fund "A"	Mutual ** Fund "B"
1939	$ 500	3.3	111	13	221	83	23
1940	2,500	15.1	243	63	1155	376	96
1941	4,500	16.6	609	80	1911	451	105
1942	6,500	18.6	630	67	1894	385	99
1943	8,500	ʼ14.4	462	56	531	293	87
1944	10,500	13.7	387	48	449	243	80
1945	12,500	11.6	342	38	269	162	68
1946	14,500	10.7	198	43	236	174	69
1947	16,500	11.2	204	43	302	190	73
1948	18,500	11.1	198	44	252	210	75
1949	20,500	11.0	198	41	259	179	69
1950	22,500	9.1	138	45	198	154	63
1951	24,500	7.8	120	47	160	129	60
1952	26,500	7.8	99	44	128	127	58
1953	28,500	7.3	99	46	129	128	59
1954	30,500	5.0	60	38	78	91	49
1955	32,500	4.1	42	42	73	68	43
1956	34,500	4.0	45	44	73	66	42
1957	36,500	4.6	50	49	68	80	46
1958	38,500	3.8	46	43	56	67	38
1959	40,500	3.2	39	34	50	57	34
1960	42,500	3.3	44	30	55	59	33
1961	44,500	2.8	42	25	43	50	28
1962	46,500	3.1	41	28	47	55	32
1963	48,500	2.8	27	27	44	51	30
1964	50,500	2.5	22	23	42	45	26
Value 12-31-64		$181,395	$440,608	$89,181	$427,427	$191,725	$123,050

*Calculated before 3–1 split.   **Adjusted for stock splits.

Note the great divergence in results that would have been realized by investing in these different companies. Back in 1939 General Motors and Woolworth were considered to be of equal investment stature. Yet $500 invested in GM at quarterly intervals since then would have produced a gain of 775% by the end of 1964, while the same investment in Woolworth did just one-tenth as well with a gain of 77.5%. Indeed, if the decline in purchasing power of the dollar is considered the value of the Woolworth holdings would be worth substantially *less* than the $50,500 invested. Moreover, since 1939, dollar averaging in the 30 Dow-Jones Industrials resulted in a gain of 240% or thrice the gain in Woolworth.

The dollar averager, then, had better be sure he has selected the right stock before embarking on such a program. As a general rule individual stocks cannot qualify as potential candidates with the exception of the Unique Profit Breakthrough companies to be discussed in detail later. The conservative approach is to operate in investment trusts which will produce less spectacular but more certain results than can be enjoyed in fast growth companies. After all, no one can be certain that today's favorite may not turn out to be a disappointing investment over the next 10 or 15 years.

In short, dollar averaging requires adequate diversification if it is to succeed with a minimum of risk.

But, in the final analysis, the real problem is this: Can you stick to *any* program for, say, a period of 10 years? If you can you are an exception to the rule. And this observation is born out by figures released by the New York Stock Exchange. 122,000 Monthly investment programs were started during the first four years the program was in effect; but more than 56,000 had been terminated during this interval. A study of the figures for each year suggests that *about 90%* of the plans started in the first year of the program had been closed out by the end of the fourth year. Yet this four year period fell during a period of generally rising stock prices and universal prosperity. When times are bad undoubtedly such programs would be abandoned even more quickly.

The success of the dollar averaging approach depends on buying more shares for a fixed number of dollars at low prices. But what about the theory of those who maintain this is all wrong and that you should only buy on a scale up?

CHAPTER 11

Averaging UP–vs–DOWN

The question is this: Is it better to buy on a scale up or on a scale down? This is an ancient and intriguing problem.

As a general rule, the novice will have a tendency to "average down." Which is to say if he buys a stock at 30 he will want to buy more at 25 on the strange theory that if it was a good buy at 30 it's an even better buy at 25.

Wrong! Wrong! Wrong! say the cagey old timers. The correct thing to do is to average up. If your stock goes down, why throw "good money after bad." Instead, if you first purchase a stock at 30 and it obligingly moves up to 35, your judgment has been vindicated. When you are "right" you should push your luck. Buy more stock at 35, still more at 40, 45 and 50. After all your cushion of profits is getting fatter all the time.

Which procedure is the best? As usual it all depends on the psychological makeup and objectives of each individual. But when buying UPB stocks both approaches are sound. In other cases, averaging down is the sounder of the two approaches for an investor while averaging up will tend to preserve the capital of a speculator from the usual rapid attrition. Why? Well, to pyramid successfully, a considerable portion of buying power must be kept in reserve so that additional purchases can be made at progressively higher prices at some future date. But the usual fate of the trader is to buy before stocks decline, hence, a trader who attempts to pyramid will actually immobilize his capital and thereby lose it more gradually.

For every successful averaging up campaign there must be hundreds of failures because the really big moves that permit it to succeed come all too seldom. And even when such a move does materialize in a stock you own rather than in one you *almost* owned, how far should you follow the rise before you stop buying and start selling? If you can answer this question go ahead and pyramid.

Nine times out of ten when you try to mastermind an averaging up campaign you will get fooled. You will be blithely buying at what turns out to be the final top. Only you won't know it was a top until most or all of your profits have evaporated. Or, you will have doubts after two or three purchases and sell out only to watch the stock proceed to double in price.

Some years ago a subscriber got sold on Pittston Co. and started buying around 50. He bought steadily on maximum margin all the way up to 84 which turned out to be the top. But at the time he was convinced the stock was going up to 150. Now several years later with Pittston around 55 he is locked into a large loss.

Pyramiding works wonderfully in theory, but like all timing systems, when practised something unexpected usually comes along that turns profits into losses. Admittedly, it sounds clever to say a stock is a better buy at 50 than at 40, but the thrifty individual will prefer to buy 200 shares at 40 rather than 100 at 40 and another 100 at 50.

This reasoning is especially valid for those who are seeking UPB stocks. The more shares you can control with limited capital the better off you are. Therefore, it follows that if a stock is a good buy at 40, it offers still better value at 30. Of course, this is not always true if meanwhile the conditions affecting the industry or company have deteriorated. In that case the stock wasn't a good buy at 40 and it should be sold as soon as the new and unfavorable developments can be assessed. But most minor price fluctuations are meaningless and usually a stock will be a better buy at a lower price. This may sound like an elementary point that should be apparent to a bright third grader, but there are a host of investors who will heatedly argue that it isn't so.

But once again, if you feel a stock offers good value at 40, buy as many shares as your program calls for without attempting to average down. If your reasoning is sound, you won't be able to buy more stock at a significantly lower price anyway. Unless, of course, a general bear trend exerts temporary pressure on your stock too. In this event, your only recourse is to rely on the positive emotions discussed in Chapter I.

About 30 years ago more intricate variations of dollar averaging became popular. Presumably, the managers of investment funds finally became aware of their inability to forecast the market (or at least to make money by doing so) and decided a robot manager would do better so the formula plan was invented.

This undoubtedly was sound thinking in some instances but it led to disaster in most cases. Not that those systems resulted in serious actual losses but too often portfolios simply became senile and failed to keep pace with even the decline in the purchasing power of the dollar due to the inflexibility of the formula plan being followed.

Results achieved by one or two of the largest college endowment funds were so bad that their formula plans were abandoned. No mechanical system can adjust to changing conditions. If it could it would have to be designed originally by someone who correctly foresaw future conditions—which would require a keener forecasting ability than is possessed by Homo Sapiens. Here again, a mechanical or semi-mechanical system is no substitute for good judgment and sound thinking.

Probably the most foolproof formula plan is one that maintains a fixed ratio of, say, 50–50 between stocks and bonds. Thus, if the value of the stock portion rises to 60% of the value of the portfolio, sufficient stocks will be sold (and bonds purchased) to return the ratio to 50–50 once again. Here, then, is a concept that, at least, makes sense. But it's suitable only for very large accounts.

Furthermore, the results obtained from this (and all) formula plans will hardly turn out to be exciting. Sooner or later the built-in disadvantages of a formula plan will outweigh the built-in advantages. Consider a seldom considered flaw in the plan just described. It's this: Bonds fluctuate in price much more than is generally realized. During one recent market downtrend, stocks—as measured by the Dow-Jones Industrials—fell 20%. Bonds —as measured by Barron's 40 bond average were off from 101.15 to 83.85 or 17%. Not much to choose from here. Moreover, when the bond market declines, *all* bonds go down as interest rates go up. Whereas, anywhere from 5 to 10% of all common stocks will move up during times when a majority of stocks are declining.

Most formula plans are geared to the market averages in one way or another—you buy and sell after certain percentage changes in the average. Numerous methods have been devised to make these plans automatically adjustable to changing conditions. However, none have succeeded. In a nutshell, none of these plans produce long-term results superior to those that could have been obtained by throwing a dart at the stock page of your newspaper and then holding the stocks so selected. In fact, this is the all important ingredient they relegate to a position of secondary importance, namely, which stocks should you buy?

So much for these variations on the dollar averaging theme. Ask a mutual fund salesman and he will tell you the answer is to invest in his wares. The idea is to let someone else—a professional—make your decisions for you. As we have seen mutual fund A did better than the averages and the salesman of that fund will quickly point out that few individuals can claim as much. True enough. But first let's look into the mutual fund claims more carefully.

CHAPTER 12

The Truth About Mutual Funds

There are two types of investment companies: The closed-end and the open-end or mutual fund. The former has a fixed sum of money to invest and the shares are traded either over-the-counter or on an exchange. There is no sales force distributing new shares. The cost of acquiring shares is the regular stock exchange commission.

In contrast, a mutual fund issues as many new shares as its sales force can sell at net asset value. The shares are not traded in an auction market but are either issued or redeemed at net asset value. When purchased the sales load averages around 8% over and above net asset value and before management fees are deducted. Sometimes a small charge is made when the shares are sold.

One of the paradoxes of the investment world is this: Why should closed end investment companies sell at a *discount* from net asset value while mutual funds are sold in much greater volume at net asset value *plus* a cost of acquisition as much as eight times more than for closed-end shares? This, in effect, means the mutual funds sell at an average premium of 8%.

Actually, of course, closed-end trusts should sell at a premium and mutual funds at a discount. The fact that they don't is a tribute to the persuasiveness of mutual fund salesmen, together with the fact that the investing public is largely unaware that closed-end trusts even exist. Unfortunately, the large wire houses and dealers who distribute mutual funds are hardly in a position to plug closed-end trusts at the expense of their mutual fund business. After all, the commission on a mutual fund sale may exceed the commission on listed investment companies *by a five or six-fold margin*.

Consider the position of a registered representative who spends the day chattering to friends and board-room loungers about baseball, the races and whether the market will be higher or lower next spring. At the end of the month, lo and behold his "gross" has amounted to only $1500 from which he may net $600—hardly enough to support that new home in Hillcrest Hanging Gardens. So the next month he is out scrounging for commissions. Bear in mind that *his* share of a mutual fund sales load may exceed his take on listed business by a margin of about *four or five to one*.

Now when a widow or orphan walks into the office with money to invest what is she most likely to wind up with? With a mutual fund and very likely with that mutual fund which charges the largest sales load. This may sound cynical but the facts bear it out. In the past, some misguided idealists have founded mutual funds which levy *no* sales charge. Most of these folded in short order because of their failure to attract customers. Even when the fund did sufficient independent advertising to attract enough customers to survive, their growth—without exception—has lagged far, far behind that of mutual funds which charge the usual 8% sales fee.

These observations should not be construed as a reflection on mutual fund salesmen or mutual funds in general. After all, the salesman's job is to sell the fund and his commission is modest in relation to the commission of, say, an insurance salesman. In addition, most investors are much better off to invest in mutual funds than to try to manage their own capital. But the fact is that closed-end trusts are almost invariably a better investment than mutual funds.

In the first place, the results achieved by closed-end companies are better *on average* than the results achieved by mutual funds. (There are, to be sure, a few exceptions). Why should this be the case? The chief reason is that the closed-end trusts with a fixed amount of capital to invest can follow a more flexible investment policy. They are not confronted with the perplexing problem of what to do with *new* capital after the market has been rising for a long time. In contrast, and most unfortunately, this is the very time that the mutual fund salesman finds it easiest to sell his merchandise.

As a result, mutual funds receive the largest sums to invest when prices are high, the smallest new capital when prices are low. The record shows that mutual fund managements tend to invest new funds as received in common stocks. Under these conditions, unless management is exceptionally able, the very nature of the mutual fund operation practically ensures a poorer performance record and lower income than could be obtained, say, from the 30 Dow-Jones Industrials.

But let's be more specific about performance records. We recently compared the performance record of 30 aggressive common stock funds to Standard and Poors

500 stock index. All capital gains payments were considered to be reinvested. During the five year period the average gain in net asset value for the investment companies was 120% compared to a gain of 181% by the 500 stock average. Only one of the mutual funds outperformed the average.

Why don't the funds do better? For one thing, a sizable segment of the stock transactions effected by mutual funds are motivated by reasons other than those dictated by investment policy. One reason is management's desire to distribute approximately the same size capital gains distribution each year. To accomplish this stocks held at a profit must be sold and the proceeds (less the gain) reinvested.

Then too, many funds have unwritten reciprocal agreements with stock exchange member firms: "If you people sell so many shares of our fund we will buy and sell so many shares of stock through your firm." There seems to be some reluctance on the part of the parties involved to throw much light on such arrangements but they exist nonetheless.

Obviously, whatever the motive behind decisions to buy and sell, mutual fund managements will do their utmost to secure the best possible performance. While the record suggests that a poor performance record doesn't act as a brake on the growth of a fund—at least not if the sales load is large enough—still it's better for all concerned to have the best possible performance record. In any event, when investment decisions are motivated by considerations other than impartial judgment the outcome is not likely to be as good as might otherwise be experienced.

In contrast, closed-end trusts are not hampered by these purely marketing considerations. Yet, they usually sell at a discount from asset value. Why? In the past, one reason was because some companies such as Tri-Continental and U. S. & Foreign Securities were highly leveraged. But today none of the larger closed-end trusts are leveraged and yet they still sell—with a few exceptions—at a discount. There is a good reason for this. Unless an investment trust manages to chalk up capital gains in excess of those registered by a representative group of top quality stocks, then the shares should sell at a discount, at least, equal to the total of management, research and other operating expenses.

One of the principal arguments advanced by mutual fund salesmen for buying their wares is that you are assured of receiving net asset value for your shares as of the day you redeem them, whereas, you can never be certain what price you will receive for a listed company since the discount (or premium) varies constantly. But why is this any advantage? In one case you can receive the net asset value, in the other the bid price on the exchange. In either case, no one knows what the price will be in advance. True, the discount at which the closed-end trust sells will vary, but then so will the net asset value of the mutual fund.

There is no appreciable advantage for either type of investment company when the sum invested is less than $100—the acquisition charges will be very nearly the same. The reason, of course, is because the New York Stock Exchange commission rates increase percentage-wise as the dollar total decreases.

But before purchasing a mutual fund think it over long

and carefully. Beware of claims or insinuations made by mutual fund salesmen. Investigate such claims thoroughly. For instance, the salesman may tell his prospective customer that if he buys the shares of the XYZ Fund today he will be eligible to receive the 90 cent dividend just declared. This is a solid reason *not* to buy since the asset value will decline by the amount of the payment. Meanwhile, the buyer will be forced to pay income taxes on the dividend which he could have avoided by waiting until the shares sold ex-dividend.

Another peculiar sales gimmick is the one that assures the buyer that the initial sales charge is the only one he will have to pay as long as he owns the shares. Thereafter, there will be no additional assessments against him—which is perfectly true. Whoever thought of this piece of sophistry was probably made chairman of the Million Dollar Round Table Club.

The new era of high pressure salesmanship which has ballooned mutual funds into a billion dollar business is exemplified by the following piece of sales literature sent to all the salesmen of one of the nation's largest and most conservative New York Stock Exchange member firms.

JOIN THE $100,000 INVESTMENT COMPANY CLUB

"We have been impressed with the number of representatives who have made sales of $100,000 or more. Others during the course of the year have recorded total sales far in excess of this figure, but have received no organization recognition other than sizable commission checks. The men and women who stand out in this phase of our business deserve, we think, continuing recognition.

Therefore, the $100,000 Investment Company Club will start its membership drive this year.

"Managers and all registered representatives are eligible for membership when retail sales during the calendar year total $100,000 or more. *Only shares of investment companies we are signed up with will count* (italic supplied).

"Instead of payment of a membership fee to the club, each new member will receive a check for $250 and a silver goblet suitably inscribed to evidence his or her club membership. Partners may become honorary members for accomplishing the same results, but with no direct benefits except the goblet."

Alas, here is another example of the penalties inflicted on the managerical class of our country.

For investors seeking maximum income combined with maximum safety, investment companies are an ideal vehicle. But for those seeking maximum growth of capital they are entirely unsuitable.

CHAPTER 13

Making Success a Reality

Up to this point we have talked a lot about what *not* to do in the stock market. So now what *do* you do? What is the one sound solution to the problem? There are two parts to it. The first has to do with timing your transactions, the second has to do with selecting the best stocks.

As for the first, the answer is simple: Remain fully invested *at all times* in those stocks which meet our selection requirements.

This sounds like a drastic proposal since speculators unanimously agree the way to "beat the market" is to buy stocks before they go up and sell them before they go down. Even long-term investors agree the thing to do is to delay buying until the bottom of a bear market which will usually coincide (they think) with the depression phase of the business cycle. Then sell at the top of the next business boom when the presumably gullible public is bidding up prices to ridiculously high levels. The astute investor, having sold, will then complacently sit on his cash and watch everyone else be ruined in the ensuing bear market and depression.

Everyone admits this classic theory is difficult to translate into practice. But few investors question its wisdom—which spells the difference between making and losing money. *Trying to buy at or near the bottom of a bear market and then sell at or near the top of a bull market is the greatest mistake of all.* Anyone who tries it ceases to be an investor and becomes an outright gambler. Why?

Because tops and bottoms can only be recognized *after* they occur and then sometimes not for a year or longer. Anyone who does identify a top or bottom at the time, does so by luck. Yet most amateur investors conclude that *they* have this magic touch. But assume you do sell near the top of a bull market. What then?

The gloom which accompanies a bear market spreads even to those apparently canny individuals who are holding cash. Inevitably, at the bottom still lower prices are anticipated. Then the market unexpectedly begins to recover and the new advance may last a year or two years without a reaction of any magnitude. With stocks becoming more expensive every day, how long should you wait before reinvesting? The answer: Usually until stocks are higher than they were when you sold.

The investor who prudently sells out to avoid a capital shrinking bear market invariably will sell far too soon since an established trend in the stock market tends to continue much longer than appears logical. As an impatient soldout bull he eventually reenters the market just before the anticipated decline actually materializes and proceeds to get whipsawed twice instead of once.

The cause of this comedy of errors can be attributed to the universal fear of being caught in a holocaust of the 1929–32, 1937–38, 1946 or 1962 variety. But *the fear of being wiped out in a major bear market leads to far more serious losses than would be caused by the dreaded event itself.*

All this leads us to one easy-to-follow conclusion. An investor should remain invested *at all times*. To succeed in the stock market, assets other than cash must be held. 99% of those who try to take advantage of market fluctuations will fail in the end. And even if we assume there *is* a 1% who succeed, they could achieve even better results by applying an entirely different philosophy of investing—the philosophy that is documented in this book.

To repeat: *Remain fully invested at all times.* By doing this you effectively eliminate the perplexing problem of *timing* transactions forevermore. You will, thereby, automatically eliminate 90% of the mistakes that inevitably lead to losses rather than profits. The other 10% of the problem involves *selection*—selection of the stocks of several companies that will, over a period of years, advance more and decline less than the market as a whole. *Unlike timing this is a problem that cannot be avoided.* Therefore, the sensible policy is to devote 100% of your in-the-market time and effort to solving it.

As already mentioned, perfect industry selection since 1915 would have (theoretically) spiraled $100 into almost $100 billion. In contrast, perfect market *timing* would have produced a gain of about $1 million or 100,000 times less than perfect selection. Here we are assuming you successfully bought and sold the Dow-Jones Average at the exact bottom and top of every major market swing.

Does this mean stock selection is 100,000 times more

important than market timing? The answer is: YES.

In a nutshell, banish the thought of timing entirely. *All commitments should be made with the intention of holding indefinitely.* That is, until the stocks held no longer qualify under the rules to be discussed shortly.

Admittedly, this requires great patience. But then patience is one of the great virtues—especially in the stock market. Because it is far easier to recognize stocks that can double or triple in price than it is to judge—in advance—how much time will elapse before it happens. Few are the investors who have not held a stock a year or two years, then sold in disgust shortly before the big move got underway.

If at this point you are thinking: "He may not mind riding a stock down in a bear market like 1929–1932 or even 1962 but I surely don't want to"; you have lots of company. In fact, too much.

The answer to this objection is two-fold. In the event of a disastrous economic and stock market collapse the selection requirements will turn negative and when a stock no longer qualifies it is automatically sold. In 1929–1932 this occurred relatively early in the decline—for many stocks it occurred in 1927 and 1928 long before the crash began.

Still another important consideration is that all stocks *don't* go down in a bear market or at least do not go down for long. Thus, the worst market break in history came in the fall of 1929. Yet in 1930, 6.5% of all listed common stocks exceeded their 1929 peaks. Included were a wide range of stocks such as, American Machine & Foundry, American Tobacco, Deere & Co., Coca Cola (a preview of its sensational advance from 17½ to 170½ between

1933 and 1937), Worthington Corp., Libby McNeil, Vanadium Corp., Standard Oil of New Jersey, Dresser Industries, American Gas & Electric and Babcock and Wilcox.

Again in 1937 and 1946 the market collapsed in the fall, yet in 1938 out of 580 leading common stocks 7.7% registered new highs. Following the 1946 crash which was far more severe in the average stock than in the Dow-Jones Averages, in 1947, 8.8% of 780 stocks bettered their 1946 highs. The problem then is to identify and concentrate in the handful of stocks that will ignore the bear market.

These almost always have UPB qualities.

During the 1929–32 holocaust, the gold stocks staged a dynamic bull market of their own. In fact, between their 1929 lows and their 1933 high this group rose an incredible 505%. True, the final stages of the advance were accelerated by the 1933 boost in the price of gold. Nevertheless, gold stocks rose to new highs in 1931 long before currency devaluation was thought of.

Again following the stock market crash of 1937 gold stocks pushed to new highs in 1938. During the final stages of the 1946–49 bear market the yellow metal shares advanced 50%, while the market averages were still declining. Gold issues, of course, differ from most stocks in that these companies prosper most during hard times (which in the past often coincided with bear markets).

But a majority of stocks which manage to counter a bear trend do so because of UPB developments peculiar to the company or its industry. During the 1920's, for instance, talking pictures blossomed out as the nation's favorite amusement and these stocks became the fashionable ones to buy. Despite the crash in 1929, movie stocks were bid up to record levels in 1930 and continued to outperform the market for many years.

Another prime example during the thirties is provided by Phillip Morris. The overnight success of the Phillip Morris cigarette created a UPB which zoomed sales from $2.6 million in 1932 to $64.2 million in 1938, while profits soared more than ten-fold. Between 1932 and 1939 Phillip Morris shares shot up from 2 to 49⅜. Even the 1937 crash caused only a momentary pause in this runaway bull market. In fact, just about every industry contributes at least one stock that moves up during a bear market because of favorable developments affecting it alone.

During the late 'thirties the aircrafts gained an even 400% as measured from their 1937 lows. Investors who switched into aircrafts when the market broke in 1937 correctly anticipated the investing public's reaction to the threat of war in Europe and the sudden influx of orders for fighter planes from Britain. Those who owned aircraft stocks went unscathed through the second worst bear market in history. Airlines also countered the bear market of the 'thirties, probably because this was the period of their greatest growth. As it turned out this superior relative strength was a prelude to the group's sensational advance during the 1942–46 wartime bull market.

During the 1946–49 bear market, the oils and coal stocks were the outstanding performers. By the spring of 1948 the group had exceeded its 1946 bull market high by a wide margin. And, as so often happens, the UPB stocks that move up during bear markets, can be relied on to rise at a faster than average rate during the next bull market. In fact, between 1949 and 1956 the oils gained 380% compared to 225% for the Dow-Jones Industrials. The reasons are plain enough. Burgeoning demand, combined with sharply higher product prices boosted earnings to record levels in 1948. In addition, investment trusts bought oil shares more heavily than any other one group, in effect, placing a floor under (but no ceiling over) prices.

A wide selection of stocks registered new highs for the 1942–46 bull market in 1947 or 1948. Some of the better known issues include: El Paso Natural Gas, International Paper, Nickel Plate R.R., Western Maryland R.R., Pittsburgh Consolidation Coal, Phelps Dodge, Newmont Mining, Minnesota Mining, Rayonier, Chicago Pneumatic Tool, Superior Oil, Joy Mfg., Dana Corp., United Fruit and Celanese. With the exception of the last two, these stocks also racked up better than average gains during the subsequent bull market.

The action of Minnesota Mining for the 20 years prior to the 1962 bear market deserves close scrutiny. MMM shares had scored new highs in just about every year as far back as the record goes. During those 20 years appreciation amounted to a spectacular 15,000%. MMM's original UPB was due, of course, to a unique new product—Scotch Tape.

Probably 1946–48 provides the best example of bullish action in a bear market. MMM was one of a handful of stocks that surged to a new high in December, 1946 only three months after the market crashed. New highs were also chalked up regularly in 1947 and 1948. Yet at a time when most stocks were making new lows, MMM looked much too high to the majority of investors. As a matter of fact, the best stocks—those that are destined to double and triple in price *always* look too high from an intrinsic value point of view, except during the very early stages of their UPB. But, finally the time arrives when the profit growth, while still good, loses its unique aspect. This happened in 1961 when MMM sold at 60 times its net income, which compared to 22 times for the average blue chip stock. Moreover, by this time, competition was intense in the pressure sensitive tape field and MMM's earnings growth had slipped from 30–40 percent a year to 10 percent so it no longer qualified as a UPB stock.

If a time came—presumably during a depression —when no stocks qualified under the UPB selection rules, then no stocks would be held and funds would be concentrated in bank savings accounts or fixed income securities until new opportunities came along.

Thus, the selection standards used also serve as a means of timing transactions, but not for the usual reasons, i.e., to sell before a bear market, or buy before a bull market.

During a severe decline such as occurred in 1962 without an economic recession of any kind, positions are not disturbed unless deterioration in the individual stocks held calls for selling anyway. In general, this did not occur in 1962 and following the panic selling in May and June UPB companies rebounded rapidly to new highs later in the year or in 1963. To illustrate, XEROX fell all the way from 170 to 90 (before splits) then soared past 400 in 1963 and 750 in 1965.

CHAPTER 14

The Unique Profit Breakthrough Concept

As we have seen, reality in the stock market takes the form of capital gains—and the bigger the better. Timing trends or trend following has been ruled out as illusionary. So correct stock selection becomes the sole objective.

Everyone in the market is looking for the big winner but only a handful know how to recognize a company that qualifies. To qualify a company must have made or be about to make a UNIQUE PROFIT BREAKTHROUGH.

In itself this is not an original concept. All of the fortune making stocks of the past have made Unique Profit Breakthroughs. But few investors are aware of the magnitude of the breakthrough or its unique quality and significance. What is needed are new standards for determining which companies qualify as UPB candidates.

What causes a common run-of-the-mill company to turn into a UPB winner?

It may be a unique and superior new product—an example: ZEROX and its dry electrostatic copying machine. It may be new management reviving a staid old company. An example: CROWN CORK & SEAL—this story later. It may be a new concept in marketing. An

94

example: ALBERTO CULVER. It may be a rich mineral find: An example: Cheap Middle East oil which proved to be a bonanza for TEXACO and other international oil companies. It may be a new type of equipment. An example: Jet propelled airplanes which fueled a UPB for the airlines. It may be a cash rich company which finds lucrative uses for the cash. Or, unusual talent for mergers. Examples: LITTON; GULF & WESTERN.

The trick is to discover UPB stocks at an *early stage* of their development, then patiently hold them and know how *long* to hold them. The most frequent opportunity will be found in a turn around situation caused by a new management team. Such a company has been stagnant for many years. Earnings have been moving sidewise or declining for many years as has the price of the stock.

When new management arrives put such a company on your "Watch" list. Watch especially to see if the new insiders start buying the stock of their new employer. (Several advisory services plus Barron's and The Wall Street Journal report on insider activities).

Sometimes you will see the stock decline after a new management has been buying heavily and you may ask, "What good does it do to know the insiders are buying if the stock declines after they buy?" The answer is this. The insiders are measuring the current price of their stock against the earning power they anticipate in a year, two years or even five years ahead. Let's say several insiders are buying XYZ stock which has been selling at 20 and earning a dollar a share. Further, assume that the profit trend has been moving sidewise in recent years. Certainly the stock looks like anything but a bargain and if several security analysts, brokers and investment advisory services place the stock on their SELL lists or if the market as a whole declines, XYZ may decline to 15 or even 10.

To the casual observer, apparently the insiders were "wrong" and those who sold at 20 were "right." But consider the position of the insiders. A new product—or process—is about to be introduced that will push earning power to $4.00 or $5.00 a share. In the eyes of the insiders the stock is cheap at 20. After all, most top management men aren't stock market experts. For all they know, the stock may not decline significantly below 20. Yet they must own stock if they are to profit from this new development. So they start buying at 20. If a decline starts, fine. They withdraw their bids and wait to see how far the stock will decline under pressure from the public who are not aware of the UPB or at least not of the great impact it will have on earnings. When the decline has carried the stock to a ridiculously low level they then resume their buying at a point where XYZ shares prove to have been an amazing bargain.

To cite but one of numerous examples. In 1955 and 1956, Lorillard (P) Company earnings fell from $1.04 to $.67 a share. The stock sank from 13 to 8. The company had merely held its own for 30 years, and few stocks looked less attractive. Advice was going out to sell Lorillard and many disgruntled impatient shareholders or traders, who said the stock "wasn't acting well," were getting out. Yet the insiders were buying the stock and in early 1957 their buying climbed to the rate of almost 30,000 shares in a single month.

A UPB was in the works.

Others guessed, but they *knew* that their new Kent filter cigarette was a runaway success. But it was not until

1958 that it was announced that 1957 earnings had tripled to $1.89 a share. By then the stock had climbed above 25. It was not until 1959 that the information was published showing 1958 earnings had more than doubled to $4.01 a share. By then the stock was selling above 40 and by 1961 it had climbed above 70.

The Lorillard success story illustrates a mature company which suddenly caught fire with a hot new product. Watch closely for these because the element of risk may be considerably smaller than in the more typical examples of smaller more speculative companies which are trying to market a new idea or product. However, sensational new product developments are far from common and their impact is difficult to time and appraise.

Another type of UPB candidate: Ailing or unprogressive companies which have just exchanged one management team for another. We will study one such example in considerable detail because a new management situation is the classical route to spectacular profits—when they are successful. Moreover, fundamentally sound companies with mediocre—or worse—management, are the rule rather than the exception. When a capable and inspired new management team takes over such a company, miracles can be worked—both in the company and the price of its stock.

A classical example is Crown Cork and Seal. Throughout the early 1950's a succession of mediocre management teams had let the company slide downhill. Crown's share of the total market for bottle caps plummeted from over one-half to less than one-third. Per-share earnings fell from $2.54 a share in 1951 to a deficit in 1957 and the company was facing bankruptcy.

Mr. John Connelly first became seriously interested in Crown in 1955 and as a competitor (he had built Connelly Container Corp. into a small but thriving business), he was thoroughly familiar with the company's problems and thought he knew how to solve them. So in 1955 he began buying stock, and in 1956, he was given a seat on the board of directors. During this period he acquired about 40,000 shares of common stock at an average price in, perhaps, the 15–18 range (this was before a four-for-one split in 1962).

By April, 1957, the board which had previously ignored Connelly's drastic suggestions for rejuvenating the company, finally gave up in despair and elected him President. In this month he bought 1,800 shares, while three other officers and directors also bought 1,800 shares. Thereafter, action came fast and furiously and the entire corporation was house cleaned. For instance, the home office staff was cut in half and by 1959, the payroll had been cut by $10 million.

In June, 1957, when Crown stock was selling around 15, Mr. Connelly took on a king-sized 28,900 shares while three other officials added smaller blocks. In July and August, he added another 19,400 shares when the stock was selling between 15 and 16. Then the market crashed and the stock promptly slid to a low of 10½ by December. During the slide Connelly and his colleagues kept right on buying and by the end of 1957, he personally held 102,700 shares in which he had a loss of perhaps $400,000 or more.

This was the crucial point at which faith and fortitude paid off. The company was running a deficit and the stock was selling at a 20-year low. Things could not have looked blacker to the average investor . . . that is, unless they knew that six different insiders had bought a total of 67,500 shares during the year just ended. And this was a typical example of a time when the insiders certainly seemed to be "wrong."

However, these men who had bought all their stock on the open market and who had severe losses did not panic like the public and sell out. They didn't even establish their losses "for tax purposes." They apparently were more interested in not running the risk of losing their positions. And, as it turned out, if they had sold in December at around 11, 31 days later they would have had to pay 15 to replace the shares sold.

Management, of course, knew that despite a deficit of $.99 a share (excluding non-recurring income) for the 12 months ending September 30, 1957, in the final quarter the company was in the black. In short, that the tide had turned. A UPB had been successfully engineered. When these figures were released in 1958 the stock was on its way a spectacular rise to 134 by December, 1961. (The split stock chalked up another new high in 1963 and 1965.) During these years net income grew at the rate of more than one dollar a share each year. According to Standard & Poors, the company's return on invested capital or "efficiency ratio," which is also sometimes referred to as the profit margin, improved faster than for any of the other 424 stocks in their Industrial Index. These figures are:

Year	1957	1958	1959	1960	1961	1962
Efficiency Ratio (%)	2.3	4.2	6.2	5.6	8.2	10.1

During 1958 when the stock tripled in price, Connelly added another 55,990 shares while other insiders bought lesser amounts. Here an important principle is involved which most investors fail to comprehend because they are either too greedy or too fearful. The insiders at Crown Cork had large paper losses at one point. Did they try "to get out even" on the recovery; or when they had a 100% or 200% profit, did they start selling? NO. They bought still more because they had bigger things in mind.

The really serious mistakes were made by investors who bought at, say, 16 in July, 1957, watched their paper losses mount with dismaying rapidity during the remainder of the year, then vowed to get out even if it ever returned to the price they paid. Equally serious mistakes were made by traders who bought at 12, and then took their 50% profit when the stock moved to 18 a few months later. As long as the UPB continues to have a favorable impact on profits, resist the impulse to take relatively small profits or to sell your stock before or during a general market decline. In retrospect, it looks easy to sell on a rally and buy back on a reaction, but invariably you lose your position in the one big winner you have and which you need to offset your other more numerous mistakes.

In 1959 and 1960, when the stock moved in a channel between 30 and 40, President Connelly and other insiders continued to methodically accumulate their stock. The heaviest buying took place in June, 1959, in the 32–34 area and again in November and December, 1960, when no less than seven officials bought 24,795 shares. By this time per-share earnings had risen to $3.15 and it was clear to them that despite the recession then underway, earnings would approach $6. a share in 1961.

As the year progressed and these earnings gains seemed more and more assured, the pace of insider buying accelerated. In January of 1961, Connelly bought another 16,125 shares. By that time the stock had reached the high 40's so at least $700,000 was involved. By May, CCK was selling in the 80's and in this month three insiders bought another 13,645 shares. In July and August six officers added another 16,770 shares, raising their holdings to 298,519 shares, or 30% of the number outstanding. At this point they stopped buying and little wonder since in August, the stock moved from 90 to above 120.

Thereafter, no significant additions were reported until the market crashed in the Spring of 1962. On that reaction, which started at 134 and ended below 80, three officers bought 18,700 shares. Then in the Fall of 1962 during the Cuban reaction, when Crown was hovering around 100, eight officials (other than the president) added stock. As noted, early in 1963 it ran up 35% to a new all-time high. What does the future hold? Well, Mr. Connelly is on record as predicting earnings will continue to rise through 1967 and as of December 1964, management held almost 1.5 million of the 4.8 million shares outstanding and after eight years are still buying their stock.

By 1964 earnings had risen to $10.12 a share (adjusted) and by mid-1965 the shares soared to another new all-time high.

The Unique Product Breakthrough

CROWN CORK is a classical example of new management revitalizing an old company. Sometimes a UPB company will originate out of a single idea for a new product. This is what produced the spectacular growth of Dymo Industries: A unique new idea for labeling. Today the Dymo System of permanent, on-the-spot labeling is seen everywhere in the world. Dymo labels, embossed in clear white letters on plastic self-sticking tapes, appear typically on office files and filing cabinets, on personal property—practically wherever there is a need for identification.

The Dymo TAPEWRITER for industrial use and the home LABELMAKER embossing tools filled a unique need for a simple, fast, permanent labeling system. Yet nothing like them had existed before.

The result: A UPB company right from the start as the following trend reveals.

	1959	1960	1961	1962	1963	1964
Sales in Millions	$.63	2.4	6.1	10.4	17.7	29.8
Earnings per share	$.02	.19	.51	.81	1.12	1.32

During the four years following the initial public stock offering, annual sales grew 12 times and net profits nearly 10 times. Small wonder the common shares sky-rocketed from 4 in 1960, to 60 early in 1964. At that point Dymo common stock was selling at more than 50 times earnings.

Let us look at another UPB company—Control Data—without going into the reasons for its unique success. At its 1963 high Control Data sold at a fantastic 175 times 1963 net income.

The question arises, when do you sell? The theory that you should *never* sell a stock as long as the reasons for buying still prevail is fine. But, you may say, "I'm practical. Theoretically, you should never sell as long as the UPB remains in effect. But from a *practical* standpoint at what point should you nail down some profit?"

In the case of Dymo, after reaching a price of 60 which was 50 times earnings, first, an antitrust suit was filed against the company; then non-recurring expenses pared the rate of earnings growth. However, neither reversed the UPB aspect of the company. Nevertheless, the stock retraced a substantial portion of its previous climb.

But in the case of Control Data, it sold at 50 times earnings when in the earliest stages of its rise. To have sold for this reason would have been the height of folly.

Theory should still prevail, but if the time arrives when you can sell a *fraction* of your position and retain all of your original investment, do it if it will satisfy a psychological need. But hold the remainder of your position as long as the reasons for the UPB remain in effect.

Unique Profit Breakthroughs can be found in the most unexpected places. Could any company be a more unlikely candidate than the Chicago & North Western Railroad Co.? Apparently, an astute lawyer named Ben Heineman did not think so. At any rate, despite huge yearly deficits he began to buy stock during the late 1950's and soon became Chairman of the Board.

In 1960, the Road reported a deficit of $14.58 a share. Yet Mr. Heineman was convinced he could rejuvenate the property and even make a profit on the losing commuter business by introducing new equipment and better service. The same philosophy worked when applied to freight service. As a result by 1963, the North Western posted a profit of $5.24 a share.

In 1965, the purchase of Velsicol Chemical Corp. was announced, which would add about $10.00 a share to net income, *without any dilution of North Western Common Stock*. This certainly represented a very tangible UPB. This combination of developments fueled a rise in NW stock from below 10 in 1962 to over 100 as this is written.

CHAPTER 15

The UPB Industry Approach

As already noted the introduction of jet aircraft fueled a UNIQUE PROFIT BREAKTHROUGH situation for the entire air transport industry. It was based on the much greater efficiency and versatility of the new jets. Another example; the perfection of color TV enabled the industry to make a UPB which produced spectacular gains for a majority of the companies in this field. But, so much for UPB's of the past. What about the present, or more accurately, the future? What industries are undergoing basic changes which could produce a dramatic impact on their collective earning power in the future?

The optics industry is one that will be transformed by a revolutionary new discovery—LASERS. Laser is short for "Light Amplification by Stimulated Emission Radiation" —and what does that mean? Briefly, ordinary light is composed of many wavelengths or colors traveling in every direction. In contrast, laser light is a concentration of one wavelength traveling in one direction. The laser will have an incredibly wide and startling variety of applications. Thus, the industry had grown from nothing to about $150 million in sales in 1966 and, perhaps, this will expand to $1.0 billion in 1970. Certainly, it would be difficult to imagine faster growth than this. And, most assuredly, some of the companies involved will translate this exciting concept into a solid UPB for their shareholders.

However, scientific discoveries such as lasers which do not have mass market application are most difficult to evaluate. In the first place, many giant corporations such as American Telephone, General Electric, IBM, DuPont, etc. are actively developing laser applications but future profits from this source will be small compared to total net income. So it appears unlikely that lasers will produce a UPB effect for such companies. There are a number of very small research-oriented firms which may very well be standing on the threshold of a UPB breakthrough. But, these companies are, for the most part, unseasoned and underfinanced. In short, the risk in these situations is far too great when even better UPB opportunities exist in major, long established industries.

UPB Industry of the 1970's?

By mid-1966 it had become evident that the construction and operation of nuclear powered electric plants would prove to be one of the great growth industries of the future. During that year the industry ordered nuclear power plants costing more than $2 billion. This was half of all the generating facilities contracted for during the year. By 1972 when all of these plants are in operation, the U.S. will have about 30 million kilowatts of nuclear generating capacity. This is *three times* the amount forecast by the Atomic Energy Commission in 1962. Late in 1966 the AEC predicted that by 1980 nuclear capacity would range between 80 and 110 million kilowatts. Here it is pertinent to point out that the AEC estimates of nuclear power growth have invariably fallen far short of what actually materialized and that some industry leaders forecast generating capacity of up to 180 million kilowatts by 1980.

Whatever the actual figure turns out to be, it is clear that an opportunity exists for investors which may never reoccur, i.e. to invest in a new industry with an extraordinary rate of growth assured by long-term contracts with the basically stable and essential electric utility industry. The reasons for this sudden demand for nuclear power stations are overwhelming.

1.   *Nuclear power costs less than fossil-fueled power and this cost advantage should widen in the future even for those nuclear reactors which are already in use. And the nuclear cost advantage is already appreciable. Thus, the giant TVA station, which will be located in the heart of low-cost coal fields will generate electricity for about 20% less than the most economical coal-fueled station could have done.*

2.   *When located in metropolitan areas nuclear reactors avoid the unsightly smoke stacks characteristic of fossil-fueled plants.*

3.   *Nuclear plants do not contribute in any way to the air pollution problems that bother so many metropolitan areas.*

4.   *Nuclear generating stations are smaller and require less land to store the vast amounts of fuel required by coal-fired stations.*

The fuel for most of the nuclear reactors now being built in the U.S. is enriched (and subsequently refined) uranium oxide (U_3O_8) or "yellow-cake". An average of five pounds of yellow-cake is obtained from each ton of uranium ore. The projected new generating stations will consume vast quantities of uranium oxide. In fact, the estimated consumption and demand for ore in 1980 will be almost double the total amount of ore discovered in the U.S. since exploration commenced during the 1940's.

In addition, it also appears possible that the demand for electric power might accelerate at a spectacular rate if the problem of air pollution in our cities worsens.

Since the chief source of smog is auto exhaust fumes,

there has been growing agitation by city planners to replace cars and trucks used only over short distances, (such as delivery, mail and milk trucks, or cars used for shopping, etc.) with electric cars and trucks. These were widely used early in this century and would be perfectly feasible. Should such a development materialize some forecasts predict the total demand for electric power might increase as much as 50% as millions of cars and trucks recharged their batteries during the night. In short, the hours of lowest power consumption today might turn out to be hours of peak load demand in the future. Such a possibility staggers the imagination. But even if the demand for electricity for recharging auto batteries increased the electric load only 10% instead of 50%, this would still mean the *rate of growth* of the electric power industry—which doubles every 10 years—would, in turn, *double*. This would, of course, further increase the already burgeoning demand for uranium.

The problem confronting an investor in mid-1966 was simply how to participate in the nuclear power boom to the greatest degree possible and with the least possible risk. What about the utility companies themselves? Might not their profit margins widen as the cost of nuclear electricity declines? Perhaps, but even if the regulatory authorities did not lower consumer rates by a similar degree, the resulting gain in profits would not constitute a valid UPB. For this to transpire would require the large scale use of the battery powered car—a development which was pure conjecture in 1966. And even if such a market did develop the firms that manufactured nuclear reactors, equipment and fuel would stand to benefit even more certainly than would the regulated utilities themselves.

Four companies dominate the nuclear plant construction competition. During 1966 General Electric got orders for 10 plants, Westinghouse for six plants, Babcock and Wilcox for three plants and Combustion Engineering for two. However, all of these companies also produce conventional generating stations which means in the future they will be building nuclear plants *instead of* fossil-fueled plants. In short, the nuclear boom may not provide the ingredients for a UPB situation unless the profit margin on nuclear plants is sharply higher than on pre-nuclear plants. This will certainly not be true in the near future.

The New Boom In Uranium

Before and during the second world war there were no known significant reserves of uranium ore in the U.S. and the development of the atomic bomb was made possible by the use of ore imported from the Belgian Congo. (The author was with the Manhattan Project at the time and was one of the scientists who worked with this uranium ore.) After the war, the AEC established a guaranteed market for uranium oxide in the form of long-term contracts first at $12 a pound and later at $8 a pound. This caused the greatest prospecting boom since the gold rush of 1849. Extensive ore bodies were discovered by or sold to the major mining companies who mined, milled and sold yellow-cake to the AEC. By the early 1960's the AEC decided it would soon have all the uranium it needed and "stretched out" the contracts to 1970 when it estimated (correctly) that demand for nuclear power would effectively replace the AEC demand. This meant lower profits for the uranium companies during the stretch-out period. Moreover, at the time the size of the future requirements by the utility industry was largely an unknown factor. It is not surprising that the uranium stocks slid to a fraction of their peak prices during the boom.

But as already noted all this has changed. In fact, by 1980 the annual dollar value of nuclear fuel being sold, which is to say uranium oxide, will probably exceed the annual dollar value of all the nuclear reactors being built. This will be true regardless of the magnitude of plant sales because the latter would be restricted by the availability of the uranium fuel. However, there will probably be no shortage of uranium by 1980 since the uranium producers all resumed extensive exploration activities during 1966. The cost of this exploration may exceed $200 million by 1980 which strongly suggests that the uranium industry anticipates higher prices as demand balloons in the years ahead.

If higher prices do materialize—say in the $8 to $10 per pound area—which would compare with an average private sale price of, perhaps $6.00–$6.50 per pound at the end of 1966—the chief beneficiaries would be the companies *which already own large, low-cost reserves of ore*. Newcomers to the industry will have to contend with the fact that a high percentage of low-cost ore, i.e. surface deposits, have already been found. In contrast, it would cost in the vicinity of $1 million in development costs to start producing uranium ore from a deposit 300 to 500 feet deep. Moreover, to go from exploration to full scale production requires, on the average, an elapsed time of seven or eight years.

Another favorable aspect of the price picture is the fact that the uranium fuel represents only about one-quarter of the cost of a reactor fuel core. As reactor construction techniques improve, the costs of fabricating cores, refining yellow-cake and so on, are expected to decline faster than the price of uranium will rise. Within a few years the fuel core may actually cost 10% to 15% less than it does today even with uranium oxide priced in the $8–$10 per pound range—and a price as high as $12 a pound is conceivable.

From the foregoing—which represents only a small fraction of the data assembled for this industry analysis —it is evident that the uranium producers should enjoy an authentic UPB which should remain intact regardless of the state of the economy. Let us assume the deflationary money-credit conditions of 1966 prove to be a temporary phenomenon and the post-war inflation is resumed and/or accelerated: There is every reason to believe that uranium would be viewed by investors as a natural resource hedge against higher prices. It is also logical to assume that the price of uranium would rise at least as rapidly as the nation's price structure in general. Actually—for reasons discussed above—it would undoubtedly rise much faster than the value of the dollar would shrink.

Conversely, if deflation and depression lie ahead, the industry that would be least vulnerable—next to gold mining—would be the electric utility industry. Moreover, it appears probable that the utility companies will want to protect themselves against a possible uranium shortage by means of longer sales contracts with the uranium producers. Then too, a period of deflation-depression would find the uranium industry in much the same position as the gold mining industry: With an assured market, declining costs are quickly translated into higher profits.

All of the major uranium companies derive income from activities other than uranium itself, though these activities are usually confined to the natural resource industries. The following report deals with such a company that has achieved a UPB in more than one phase of its business. It was prepared for the management of a major mutual fund and is reproduced to demonstrate the type of research required to document an authentic UPB situation. About one-third of the original report has been omitted because of space considerations. This company seemed like an ideal subject since it is a major supplier of *both coal and uranium* to the utility industry. The name of the company has been disguised since the purpose of this book is to demonstrate basic investment principles, rather than to make investment recommendations.

AN ANALYSIS OF THE XYZ MINING COMPANY
July 1966
SUMMARY AND CONCLUSIONS

XYZ shares now sell around 35 or less than 12 times estimated earnings of $3.05 for the current fiscal year. Looking ahead to fiscal 1970 we visualize a minimum of $6.50 per share which at 15 times earnings—a more normal multiplier for a company of this stature—would be equivalent to a price of around 100 for the stock.

This dynamic earnings trend is solidly based on UNIQUE PROFIT BREAKTHROUGHS that have been made or are about to be made in several different phases of the company's operations. These UPB's are the result of an enterprising young management team who are thoroughly imbued with the UPB concept and who had the vision many years ago to take far reaching steps that are now beginning to pay off in a big way. With vast natural resources sold under long-term contracts, we think the common stock of XYZ Mining will provide an effective hedge against either further inflation or deflation resulting in reduced business activity.

SUMMARY OF OPERATIONS
Years ended October 31

	1961	1962	1963	1964	1965
Revenues (millions)	$81.1	$84.3	$77.8	$59.9	$89.3
Pre-tax margin	16.0%	14.2%	10.4%	15.0%	17.0%
Net income (millions)	$ 9.8	$ 9.3	$ 7.1	$ 7.3	$11.0
Depreciation & depletion (millions)	$ 6.4	$ 6.8	$ 6.9	$ 6.1	$ 4.9
Earnings per share (a)	$ 2.27	$ 2.17	$ 1.65	$ 1.70	$ 2.56
Dividend per share (a)	$ .78	$ .86½	$ .90	$ .95	$ 1.15
Return on equity	17.2%	14.5%	10.6%	10.4%	14.4%

(a) Adjusted for stock dividends of 2% paid in 1960, 1961, and 1962, and 100% in 1963.

CAPITALIZATION

	Book October 31, 1965		Market June 10, 1966	
Long-term debt	$ 29,304,000	28%	$ 39,304,000	20%
Common equity	$ 76,356,000	72%	$163,409,000	80%
Total	$105,660,000	100%	$202,713,000	100%

10/31/65		
Current assets	$ 26,896,256	Current Ratio
Current liabilities	$ 19,658,287	1.4
Working capital	$ 7,237,969	

History 1900-1965

In 1900, XYZ Mining began operations as a domestic contractor and railroad builder and shortly thereafter built 700 miles of Western Pacific Railroad track (including the famous 75 mile section through California's Feather River Canyon). With the completion of this job, similar projects followed and railroad construction became the company's primary activity for the next two decades. In the early 1920's, participation in foreign ventures was initiated with the construction of 100 miles of railroad track in Mexico. In 1931, XYZ was one of the largest companies involved in constructing Hoover Dam. Since that time XYZ's activities have included such projects as the San Francisco-Oakland Bay Bridge, Bonneville Dam, Grand Coulee Dam, the Alcan Highway and the St. Lawrence Seaway.

A major step leading to XYZ's present day diversification was taken in 1942 when the company decided to utilize its earth moving skills to perform contract mining operations for mineral property owners. This experience led the Company to find and develop its own mineral properties; within a decade XYZ was the leading independent iron ore producer in the West. In 1953, the company launched its overseas mining operations with the construction and operation of subsidiary A's iron ore facilities in Peru, which has since developed into one of the largest iron ore producers in the world. To bring about shipping economies and improve service, shipping subsidiaries B and C were formed to market and transport ore.

XYZ entered the uranium field in 1957 through its interest in Lucky Mc Uranium Corporation. Merged with XYZ in 1960, Lucky Mc processes its own ore and performs milling services for ores from XYZ's properties and from other producers.

With the opening of its Navajo coal mine in Arizona during the spring of 1963, the Company added a new chapter to its mining history. Under a long term contract XYZ provides coal for Arizona Public Service Company's Four Corners steam power plant. As other utility companies install generating capacity to accommodate the Southwest's growing power requirements, XYZ will be able to provide additional coal tonnage from the huge Navajo mine reserve. In addition to the Navajo mine the Company has other coal deposits in Utah and Arizona. Moreover, to assure the availability of future resources, XYZ's Mineral Development and Geology Department maintains an exploration program covering several continents.

Land development activities began shortly after the close of World War II with the planning and construction of large scale housing developments. By 1954, the Company had undertaken nearly 30 major developments in principal growth centers throughout the western states. In several instances XYZ's land activities have entailed the acquisition and development of land requiring some degree of reclamation with earth moving equipment or high capacity hydraulic dredges. Today, as a result of a broad real estate program, the Company is developing a number of residential communities, senior citizens residences, and industrial parks throughout California. Other properties are being held for future development or investment.

Mining Operations

By far the most important of XYZ's operations today are its mining activities; these include iron ore, copper, uranium, and coal, with iron ore presently the most significant. Since 1943, XYZ has expanded its mining operations into a fully integrated organization now operating on three continents. The Company's activities, both for its own account and on a contract basis, range from geological explorations, metallurgical testing, and developing of new ore bodies, to process engineering and design, construction of plant facilities, mine and mill operations, marketing and shipping.

Iron Ore

In the Cedar City, Utah area, XYZ mines and markets iron ore from several of its own properties and conducts contract operations for the Colorado Fuel & Iron Corporation.

The Columbia-Geneva Steel Division of the United States Steel Corporation is the largest customer for ore from XYZ's Cedar City reserves, purchasing a substantial portion of total production under a contract which runs until 1975. Construction of a $1.3 million beneficiation plant was completed in 1961, and a mobile plant for processing of alluvium deposits began operation in 1964.

Development of the Mount Goldsworthy iron ore deposits, located near the northwest coast of Australia, was awarded to a consortium composed of XYZ (⅓), Cyprus Mines (⅓), and Consolidated Gold Fields (⅓). Exploration and mineral development work, completed in 1963, indicated a large deposit of commercially marketable iron ore.

In December 1964, representatives of Japanese steel mills agreed to purchase 16.5 million tons of ore from

Mount Goldsworthy over a seven year period. Shipments commenced in May of this year at the rate of 1½ million tons a year to be increased to 2½ million tons in 1967. It is estimated that this project could develop earnings in the area of 40c an XYZ share when it reaches its peak in 1968.

XYZ and another company control 5,460 acres of mining lands near Dayton, Nevada, which contain one of the largest proven iron ore reserves in the western United States. Developed ore reserves of the main ore body, minable by open-pit methods, total 44,240,000 tons and additional ore reserves of about 15,000,000 tons lie below this. Outlying ore bodies, not yet fully developed, add about 6,000,000 tons to the Dayton reserves.

Subsidiary A

XYZ owns a 43% equity interest and a 50% voting interest in Subsidiary A, which is one of the world's major iron ore producers. A has been mining iron ore since 1953, when it was formed by XYZ and another company to develop and mine an extensive deposit in Southern Peru. Located near deep water port sites and having a downhill mine-to-port haul, year-round operating climate and favorable stripping ratios, A is one of the world's lowest cost export-ore deposits. Since its formation, A has generated profits in excess of $56 million and paid dividends of $18.5 million.

A's reserves are derived from two sources: concessions granted by an agency of the Peruvian Government and the wholly-owned LaJusta properties. The combined properties extend over 600,000 acres. Although the Government concession continues until 1982 and may be extended by agreement, the fee deposits alone assure continued mining operations well beyond that date. A's proven reserves of ore, based on closely spaced development drilling and calculated to a depth of about 500 feet, are in excess of 200 million tons and have an average iron content of better than 56%. In addition, there are indications of huge quantities of probable reserves which exceed the proven reserves. The depth of the primary ore body remains undetermined; drill holes more than 1,000 feet deep have failed to reach the bottom of the ore deposits.

In July, 1960, Subsidiary A embarked on an expansion program. The initial stages involved the addition of crushing and stockpiling facilities, a two-mile downhill transport conveyor and interconnecting roadway network between the mine and San Nicolas, beneficiation facilities, and a modern deepwater pier construction. Additional expansion provided magnetic separation and pelletizing plants and greater power, storage, and ore processing capacity.

Last year the company decided to construct an additional pelletizing unit having a production capacity of 2 million tons per year. This latest expansion will be completed this summer and will enable A to process its large ore reserves and to produce premium quality, high-grade sinter and pellet products for the Peruvian steel industry and a competitive world market.

Long-range planning, dependent upon the nature of the international iron ore market and the political stability of Peru, envisions future improvements and expansion enabling A to supply high quality iron ore products to its expanding foreign markets.

Subsidiary B

XYZ owns a 43% interest in the equity stock and a 50% interest in the voting stock of Subsidiary B whose principal role is the marketing and transportation of Subsidiary A iron ore. In the future B will perform a similar function to the iron ore production from Mount Goldsworthy in Australia.

This affiliate enjoys a unique advantage in the shipping industry in that full utilization of its ships is assured by the long-term iron ore delivery contracts between Subsidiary A and various steel producers throughout the world. Generally, a chartered fleet is employed to transport ore under sales agreements of shorter duration.

During 1965 Subsidiary B's fleet and 108 chartered ships moved approximately 65 billion ton miles of iron ore and other bulk cargoes; the primary movement was the transportation of iron ore between Subsidiary A's deep water shipping port and its markets in Asia, Western Europe and North and South America. Nearly one-half of the iron ore tonnage shipped last year was delivered to steel makers in Japan and more than one-third went to German and other European consumers. The balance was shipped to the United States, Argentina and Peru.

Since its incorporation in 1953, Subsidiary B's earnings (including those of its wholly-owned Subsidiary C) have totalled in excess of $44 million and dividends of $3 million have been paid to its shareholders.

The ships of Subsidiary B transport Subsidiary A ore and other bulk cargoes throughout the world. The vessels owned by this subsidiary of Cia. San Juan, S.A. are listed below:

Vessels	Capacity—(DW tons)
San Juan Prospector	71,308
San Juan Pathfinder	71,205
San Juan Pioneer	70,254
San Juan Trader	62,000
San Juan Merchant	49,520
San Juan Traveler	49,437
Harvey S. Mudd	31,662
Allen D. Christensen	31,491
	436,877

Subsidiary C ships, with an original cost in excess of $62,000,000 were especially designed for iron ore trade, and its newer ships are among the largest combination ore-oil carriers in the world. Subsidiary A was the first to build and economically use super-sized ore/oil carriers capable of lifting their full deadweight in either ore or oil. The company is now one of the leading designers and owners of the largest ships used as multi-purpose carriers making Subsidiary A one of the most successful international marketers of heavy bulk products in the world. C has also ordered a 91,000-ton ore carrier to be delivered in 1967 which will be substantially larger than any other ore carrier in existence today. In addition to owned vessels, C also operates 12 large combination vessels under long term charters, three of 55,000-ton capacity having been added at the end of 1965.

Copper

Ninety-two percent of the Western World's copper is consumed and developed in this country. The largest single use of copper in the United States is electrical products accounting for about 28% of the total. Next comes machinery and industrial equipment with about 20%, then building and construction at 19%, and finally transportation, the bulk of which is automotive, at around 13%. Manufacturers who need additional copper were recently paying almost twice the producer price in some of the various outside markets. Producers' prices in the United States now at 36 cents per pound, are still several steps above the 31 cent level which had remained unchanged for almost four years until early 1964. London Metal Exchange spot prices recently reached a record of 80 cents because of the Chilean strike and the threat of reduced supplies from Southern Rhodesia. The seriousness of the short supply is amplified by the fact that most of the government's 200,000 tons of copper it intended to sell is not surplus but part of the strategic reserves. Thus, copper shortages developed in early 1964 as a result of rising industrial usage will probably continue despite the near capacity production by all producers throughout the world.

It is interesting to note that XYZ Mining owns a 25% equity in Pima Mining Company, which since December 1956 has been engaged in open pit mining and milling of the Pima copper deposits located some 20 miles south of Tucson, Arizona.

Profits from Pima in 1965 amounted to $4,800,000 compared with $3,000,000 in 1964. In April 1965, the Directors of Pima Mining approved a plant expansion from the then rated capacity of about 6,000 tons of ore daily to 18,000 tons of ore per day. Financing of the $20,000,000.00 project was provided by Pima's self generated funds and a $14,000,000, 5% loan. This larger mill which went into operation last month will make it profitable to process lower grade ores from the area adjoining the present pit. Moreover, it will extend the life of the mine well into the 1980's. With the completion of this expansion program, Pima's 1966 output should be roughly twice that of 1965, which along with lower production costs and increased copper prices, should result in considerably higher earnings for Pima this year. Moreover, because of the discovery of additional ore reserves, Pima is presently investigating the possibility of expanding its present plant capacity of 18,000 tons to 30,000 tons of ore per day.

Coal

The United States has the world's largest reserves of bituminous coal, estimated to be 3.4 trillion tons. During the latter part of the 1950's, bituminous coal was widely regarded as a sick industry. Because of the shift from steam to diesel locomotives it had lost its largest single market. Other technological changes reduced the demand for coal in the steel industry, in the home heating market and in various manufacturing operations. The only stable market expansion was in the area of electric utilities. Recently, however, because of technological innovations, coal has made a remarkable comeback. It is now in a position to compete strongly with existing fuels and has a cost advantage over other available fuels which it did not have 15 years ago.

New technologies in EHV (extra high voltage) transmission have been developed, making it possible to transmit electricity over long haul distances at reduced cost. Known as "coal by wire", EHV has made it possible to locate power plants at the mine-mouth. By thus eliminating long haul coal transportation costs, coal will be placed in a much better competitive position.

Coal demand is expected to increase about 100% between 1965 and 1975 with the greatest demand coming from the electric utilities. The market for electrical energy grew at the rate of 6% per year from 1960 to 1965. Utilities will create a coal market of 500 million tons by 1980, which is about double the total utility demand in 1964.

Moreover, there is a trend toward super-sized generating plants, which by 1980 will be as large as 5.5 million kilowatts.

Navajo Power Project, New Mexico

The company's Navajo mine, located on the Navajo Indian Reservation in the northwest corner of New Mexico, is one of the largest low-cost thermal energy deposits of bituminous coal in the world. With estimated reserves of over 750 million tons of strippable coal, this fuel supply could provide the energy for the annual production of 5½ million kilowatts of electricity for more than 35 years.

In an extensive survey of this area made between 1953 and 1955, XYZ's geologists located a coal deposit large enough to justify a large-scale mining operation. Although there was no local market for coal the company considered the feasibility of a power-generating facility near the mine site for the transmission of electrical energy to some of the southwest's population centers.

XYZ also applied to the State of New Mexico for water rights subsequently granted, and, in 1957, a long-term mining lease, embracing 24,320 acres, was signed by the Navajo Indians and ratified by the Department of the Interior. The lease provides for royalty payments to the Navajos for each ton of coal mined and additional payments on certain other minerals, if found and developed.

Early in 1963, culminating a decade of planning, negotiations and developments, XYZ commenced coal production and delivery under a long term fuel supply agreement with Arizona Public Service Company. The basic contract covering a period of 35 years, with an option to renew for an additional 15 years, will provide coal for the utility's Four Corners steam powered generating facility where it now has three generating units.

The lease, covering 38 square miles, provides for the mining of one or more coal seams lying below 20 to 120 feet of overburden. The stripping of this material is accomplished with a huge "walking" dragline, having a 40 cubic yard bucket and a 250 foot boom. At current production rates, coal is removed by two 11 cubic yard coal shovels.

The tonnage required by Arizona Public Service represents only a portion of the Navajo Mine reserves. With more than 600 million tons of coal still uncommitted, the company hoped to develop new markets in order to realize the full potential of this fuel deposit.

There seemed to be little interest in coal among western utilities (other than APS) until about two years ago. At that time, a group of the 15 members of the Western Energy Supply & Transmission Associates, (Arizona Public Service Company, El Paso Electric Company, Nevada Power Company, Public Service Company of Colorado, Public Service Company of New Mexico, San Diego Gas & Electric Company, Sierra Pacific Power Company, Southern California Edison Company, Tucson Gas & Electric Company, Utah Power & Light Company, Los Angeles Department of Water & Power, Pasadena Municipal Light & Power Department, Glendale Public Service Department, Burbank Public Service Department and Imperial Irrigation District), formed a planning group called WEST Associates with the objective of providing for the long term power needs of the West.

Their association had been encouraged by recent power shortages in the West and the ever present threat of Federal power generation to supply such shortages. This group indicated the need for 36 million kilowatts of new generating capacity in the West over a twenty year period. The study also indicated that coal could well be a preferred fuel for much of this capacity. It was also estimated that the group might consume 10 million tons of coal a year by 1971, 50 million tons by 1978, and 105 million tons a year at the termination of the program.

Construction will start this year on a new plant to be owned by members of WEST Associates. This plant, which will be located near the Navajo mine, will have a capacity of 1,510,000 kilowatts and fuel requirements of 6 million tons per year. If fuel agreement negotiations presently in progress are successfully concluded and the plant is fully operational by 1969, XYZ's coal production at the Navajo mine will have increased to an annual rate of 8.5 million tons, making Navajo the largest coal mine in the world. Some idea of the projected size of WEST can be obtained by comparing it to other well known electric power projects; its capacity will be more than three times the present capacity of Tennessee Valley Authority, it will be equivalent to 18 Grand Coulee dams and have the capacity of almost 17 High Aswan dams.

The profitability of XYZ's coal operation has not been revealed, but it is generally felt that a skilfully conceived project of this nature could develop earnings of 60c to 70c a ton after initial royalty payments to the Navajo Indians of 15c a ton. Thus, annual earnings of $1.25–$1.50 a share could be generated by 1969 based on the sale of

8½ million tons of coal. If the increased power demands projected by WEST Associates are realized in the next 5 to 10 years it would not be unlikely that the potential annual production of some 22 million tons would be fully utilized. On this basis, annual earnings *from Navajo alone* would be somewhere in the area of $3.00–$4.00 a share. So XYZ's UPB should be valid for many years to come.

It should be noted here that the future use of atomic power will make greater headway in other parts of the country where such large low cost deposits of coal are not economically available and where air pollution presents a problem.

The Company's western coal reserves total well over one billion tons. Near the town of Craig in northwest Colorado, the Company controls a sizable reserve of coal suitable for electric power generation, and also has a large water right and storage permit in the nearby Yampa River. It also controls strippable steam coal deposits in southern Utah near the town of Kanab. These reserves are well situated to serve the southern California energy market. In addition to its proven deposits, XYZ is actively investigating other reserves of strippable and underground coal.

Coking Coal—Queensland, Australia

In 1960, XYZ Development Company, a wholly owned subsidiary, began a preliminary investigation of Australian coking coal properties, and in the two years following carried out an extensive drilling program to locate strippable deposits of coking coal. As a result of these efforts XYZ now controls some 2500 square miles of potential coal lands under Authority to Prospect and, near the town of Blackwater on the Queensland Railroad, has developed a substantial reserve of quality coking coal.

In 1965, XYZ Development Company signed a letter of intent with the Japanese steel industry for the sale of 13½ million tons of coking coal from the Blackwater area over a 10 year period. The contract is conditional on the satisfactory testing of a bulk sample, now nearing completion in Japan. Production is scheduled in 1968 at a rate of one-half million tons annually, increasing to 1½ million tons by 1971.

Uranium

Located in the Gas Hills district of Wyoming, Lucky Mc is one of the world's most efficient open pit uranium mines. Its processing plant has a daily rated capacity of 1,200 tons. XYZ's contracts with the Atomic Energy Commission, originally to have been terminated in 1966, have been extended through 1970. Although the new program will reduce anticipated profits for the short-term, it will produce greater total revenues. With production at the rate prevailing under the new government program, minable reserves controlled by Lucky Mc are sufficient to support many years of uninterrupted production.

Until recently all uranium production had been contracted for by the United States Government. However, XYZ has recently announced a contract to sell approximately 750,000 pounds of uranium oxide concentrate to a Swiss utility to fuel its 350,000 kw. plant now under construction at Beznan, Switzerland. It is expected that the first delivery will be made during the last half of 1967.

Another agreement has just been announced for the sale of uranium oxide concentrate to a group of Swedish utilities. The latest agreement calls for 1968 deliveries of from 765,000 to 840,000 pounds of uranium oxide. These two contracts are only the beginning of a growing world-wide demand for uranium.

Beyond 1970, XYZ will still have substantial reserves and with reduced costs which are believed to be competitive with any domestic producer, the Company should be in an excellent position to participate in the growth of the nuclear power industry. Their optimism for the strength of this future market is underscored by the Company's re-entry into uranium exploration. An increasing number of utilities have announced plans for nuclear generating facilities and it now appears that the public interest might justify a federal purchase program after 1970.

Land Development

XYZ Mining has been able to employ its skills in the field of earth moving to considerable advantage in land development. Over the past decade, the Company has developed a wide variety of residential and industrial properties. These have been located primarily in the State of California, but activities have also extended to a number of other West Coast states.

For the past several years, however, property liquidations have exceeded new land acquisitions. This reflects the growing difficulty of obtaining land in California at reasonable prices. Management feels that in order to make a real estate operation attractive, the land must have the potential to double in price approximately each seven years. Under these circumstances, while real estate will doubtless continue to be a source of earnings in the foreseeable future, this phase of the business is expected to decline in relative importance in the years ahead.

Construction and Dredging

Construction activities account for about two-thirds of the Company's total revenues, but have made only a minor contribution to earnings in recent years. In 1963 and 1964, construction activities actually resulted in an operating deficit, primarily because of a major loss on the Round Butte hydroelectric project in Oregon. With a number of other major contracts working out well, construction was slightly profitable in fiscal 1965 and should do at least as well in the current fiscal year. Eventually, the almost universally unprofitable experience of the heavy construction industry may cause some marginal competitors to drop out of the business and result in a more realistic approach to bidding.

For the present at least, the major contribution of the construction part of the business is intangible. Construction operations involve much of the same know-how required in mining and often provide entrees into profitable mineral ventures.

The Company has three dredges, two of which are among the largest in the world. In contrast to construction, dredging operations have been generally profitable and have potential for some modest growth.

Dividends and Stock Ownership

Cash dividends have been paid every year since 1931. In 1965, the Company raised its quarterly dividend from

20c to 25c a share and, in addition, paid a year end extra of 15c a share. With excellent prospects for higher earnings it does not seem unreasonable to expect an increase in either the extra or regular dividend some time this year.

Of the 4,300,239 shares of common stock outstanding, approximately one-half are held by, perhaps, 100 individuals associated with or close to the Company. Although the stock is traded in modest volume O.T.C. there are frequent opportunities to obtain—or dispose of—reasonably good sized positions without causing a substantial change in the price. Management does not intend to list the stock on any exchange at the present time.

Current Earnings and Longer Term Prospects

Prospects for the current fiscal year are excellent. For the first half ended April 30, 1966, earnings rose to $1.34 a share from $1.25 in the corresponding period last year. Not only have the copper and iron ore mining facilities been expanded substantially but slightly higher prices are anticipated for the balance of the year. These developments along with greater income from Australia should result in a record level of earnings this year, i.e., somewhere in the area of $3.00 a share.

As indicated in the net income figures below, the company reveals only the income from its Subsidiary A, B and Pima operations. We believe, however, that there is sufficient information to make a reasonable guess as to where the balance of net income is derived. On this basis we can break down the net income to arrive at $2.56 a share earned last year. We also indicate where possible increases (copper, iron pellets and shipping) and decreases may occur this year and in later years.

It is admittedly a hazardous and somewhat presumptuous task to make such projections but where such long term contracts and vast ore reserves are concerned, we believe it is not an unreasonable thing to do. Moreover, in the case of XYZ's coal income, we believe our assumptions concerning its profitability are quite conservative. In addition, there will in all probability be a considerably greater demand for coal from WEST Associates before 1975.

NET INCOME
(in thousands)

	10/31/65	%	Estimated 10/31/66	%	Projected 10/31/70	%
Copper	$ 908	8.4	$ 2,000*	15.6	$ 2,500*	9.2
Uranium	2,000*	18.2	2,000*	15.6	3,000*	10.7
Iron Ore	2,726*	24.5	3,600*	27.8	9,300*	33.1
Coal	1,600*	14.4	1,600*	12.5	7,800*	27.8
Shipping	1,749	16.0	2,200*	17.0	4,000*	14.2
Other	2,033*	18.5	1,500*	11.5	1,400*	5.0
Net Income	$11,016	100.0%	$12,900*	100.0%	$28,000*	100.0%
per share	$2.56		$3.00*		$6.50*	

*Estimated

As indicated above, income from both Subsidiary A and its shipping affiliate are expected to increase over the years as the worldwide demand for iron ore grows and as the large bulk carriers develop greater markets around the world. With its new beneficiation and pelletizing facilities this subsidiary now has one of the lowest cost iron pellet operations in the Western Hemisphere. Moreover, it has prodigious ore reserves, and the largest and most efficient fleet of multi-cargo ships in the world.

These ships, which have revolutionized the cargo carrying industry, were designed and developed by Subsidiary A's forward looking management.

In the case of copper, we can only say that it would not seem unreasonable to expect some eventual price increases in the United States. Such increases—along with greater mine capacity—can only be regarded as favorable to XYZ's earnings.

The electric utility industry, coal's largest customer, will experience unprecedented growth within the next ten years, particularly in the Southwestern part of the United States. Studies indicate that power requirements in this area will be so great that both coal and uranium will have to be utilized. Whereas generating capacities of 100,000–500,000 kilowatts were considered sizable not long ago, new plants of 1,500,000 kw's and even 5,000,000 kw's are in the planning stage today. With such a tremendous demand we expect the Navajo mine, which also has access to a large supply of water (essential to steam generation), to be operating at a substantially greater rate in the next five years.

In the case of uranium, there is a growing demand throughout the world for electrical energy. In the years ahead this demand cannot be met with the traditional coal and gas generated steam and hydro plants. The use of atomic power, which is now economically feasible in certain areas of the world, can only increase—and probably at a very rapid rate in terms of kilowatts generated. However, less than 1% of today's electricity is generated by nuclear power. Some projections for nuclear generation (as revealed in the recent National Power Survey) estimate that atomic power's percentage of installed capacity will be 19% by the year 1980.

One of the most interesting questions posed today for a uranium producer such as Lucky Mc is that of uranium reserves. Although the Lucky Mc reserves are reputedly one of the largest in the industry it should be clear that reserves depend to a great extent on the price of uranium. With limited world-wide reserves available at present prices, it would seem only reasonable to expect higher future uranium prices. This, of course, would create greater reserves as the demand increases.

In addition to the growing mining activities mentioned above are, of course, the Queensland and Mt. Goldsworthy operations in Australia. These coal and iron ore activities should continue to grow at a good rate over the next decade.

Despite the fact that it is the most unpredictable portion of XYZ's business, construction earnings can be expected to show improvement in the years ahead. More reasonable bidding throughout the industry and a greater use of "cost plus fixed fee contracts" should enable XYZ to derive a more satisfactory return on its construction activities.

Land development will tend to decline as a percent of the Company's operations because of the Company's desire to emphasize its more profitable and stable mining operations and because profit opportunities in real estate are not as common as in the past.

In general then, the longer term prospects for the company's diversified interests are indeed bright. Under the direction of an extremely able management, the Company has established the foundation for a substantial and sustained increase in earnings. As the investment community re-assesses XYZ's intrinsic value and earning capability, we believe its common stock will be accorded a multiple more in line with that of other diversified companies whose earnings are also growing at a very rapid rate. Since an important part of its future earnings will be derived from long term contracts with the public utility industry, this should add a considerable element of stability to its operations which is lacking in other large scale mining companies. In view of this very intriguing growth potential, and considering the modest downside risk, we consider the common stock an outstanding vehicle for capital appreciation over the next several years.

CHAPTER 16

How To Be Right More Often

A number of objective studies have been carried out by impartial agencies in an effort to determine the accuracy of stock market forecasters. All such studies have indicated that forecasters *as a group* are right about 50% of the time. Now a scientific study isn't needed to come up with this answer. Take any large group of recommendations, or any large group of investors, about 50% will be right and 50% wrong over the long pull (if this was not the case, a free market for securities would soon disappear).

But it stands to reason that among the forecasters who were right, some were right considerably more than 50% of the time. Some advisors will be "in tune" with the market for long periods, or will have a knack of consistently locating UPB stocks and then staying with them. So if you're out to beat the market be sure you get your advice from one of these lucky few. But watch out. Sooner or later even these fortunate forecasters will slip "out-of-gear" and will be wrong for long periods. In short, *in the long run* no one will accurately predict the future action of the stock market as a whole more than 50% of the time—notwithstanding claims and proofs to the contrary.

133

Because, as we have seen, "timing" market transactions is an illusion.

Need we be discouraged by this revelation? Not at all. The fact is, sound investment advice begins where market forecasts leave off. The mature advisor knows that to ensure superior results he must first eliminate the urge or need to foresee future market fluctuations.

Now that we have eliminated the need for a crystal ball, what attributes are essential in a superior investment advisor?

The answer boils down to this: First, he must have integrity and sound judgment. Next, he must be independent in his thinking, free to pursue a course of action which he—contrary to the opinion of others—is convinced is correct. Finally and most important of all, is his investment *philosophy*. He must be able to distinguish between reality and illusion. He must have the ability to sense a UPB situation before other analysts do and then confirm it by an exhaustive analysis of the company. Such an individual will usually be operating for himself. Or, he may be an employee or partner of any type of firm in the investment business. In the latter case, it is important to realize that sound advice is more likely to emanate from some types of firms than from others.

If the principal business of an investment firm is selling securities then chances are that some of the employees of that firm are not in a position to render impartial investment advice. If the principal business of the firm is borrowing and lending money, chances are you should go to that firm for these services only—not for investment advice. Such a conclusion seems obvious and it in no way reflects on the integrity or ability of individuals in those firms who may attempt—often reluctantly—to also function as investment advisors.

Recently, a prominent stock broker whose firm is a member of the New York Stock Exchange, stated that today the customer regards his broker as his investment advisor and would be lost without his help. Possibly this is one reason so many people do badly in the market. A broker's function should be to execute orders as efficiently as possible for his customers and to keep him advised about developments which may affect his holdings. If the salesman has any business at all, these chores will keep him fully occupied. How can he possibly find time to do the analytical work required to make well balanced decisions about what his client should or should not own?

Yet the usual broker-customer relationship leads to illusionary conversations something like this one:

Customer: "What's a good buy today, Dick?"

Dick: Who hasn't the faintest idea and why should he have? "Well, our research department says Central Railroad of New Jersey plans to develop the land over their Jersey City Station. They estimate that Central's real estate is worth $20 a share. With the stock currently selling at $20, this means that you get the whole railroad free when you buy the stock. You know how right Jack has been on the market? Well Jack thinks Central will sell for 50 within a year."

Customer: "I've never liked Jersey Central." (This statement suggests he doesn't need any advice at all.)

Dick: "Well what about Fruehauf Corp.? The President of the company has just predicted that sales will jump from $275 million last year to $300 million this year. If so, earnings should at least double. This is a dynamic growth company and at 38 the stock looks like a real bargain."

Customer: "You know I've always wanted to buy Fruehauf. My brother uses their trailers in his trucking business and swears by them. Let's buy 500 shares.

Dick: (hopefully) "Shall we put the order in at the market?"

Customer: "Let's get a quote." (The quote comes back 37¼ bid, offered at 38.) "Why don't you bid 37 for the 500 shares."

Dick: (again hopefully) "Shall we enter an open order?"

Customer: "No make it a day order."

At the end of the day he hasn't bought the stock, doesn't reenter the order, and so no harm is done. Chances are the bulk of the advice rendered by customer's men resembles the advice that Dick gave his customer. It's advice from second hand sources, designed to get the customer to take action.

Too many salesmen get their ideas from the daily market letters issued by every broker. All told, there are about 300 of these daily tip-sheets distributed free of charge. After writing market letters for many years, we feel for this hardy breed. Most of the writers are attempting (1) to predict the future trend of the market and (2) pick stocks for their readers that will go up and go up fast. The former can only be accomplished by an unusually gifted (or lucky) person which immediately eliminates 98 out of 100 market letter writers.

Thus, 98 seers are confronted with a bit of a problem. When you know that about three times out of four you are going to be proved wrong almost before your letter is in print, you naturally look around for some way to cushion the blows. The obvious solution is to write a market letter that can be interpreted as either bullish or bearish, or better still, one that can't be comprehended at all. Here are typical quotations from a few of the most widely circulated market letters distributed by some of the biggest and most respected names in Wall Street.

1. "Even though business as a whole may decline through the early part of the coming year, a number of industries may buck the trend. The best approach is to presume it will be a trendless market similar to last year and as far as the averages are concerned not more than 10% above or below present levels."

Now most of us have become so hypnotized by reading market letters that we nod our heads and say "this makes sense." But does it? Translated into English this paragraph would read something like this. "The market will either go up or down, take your choice. Some industries will advance, others will decline." Which after all deserves our respect because it's at least honest.

2. "Much will be told about the medium-term future of the market by its action over the next several days. If the decline can be stemmed at a level even moderately above the October low, a subsequent rally to a point measurably above recent prices will remain a definite possibility. But the chance of a materially greater decline seems at least as great."

While this one is a little more difficult to translate the message is quite simple: "If the market is going up it will go up, if it is going down it will go down."

In this morning's mail came another illuminating bit of market analysis: "Obviously a sufficient base of confidence has not been formed to support a near-term sustained rise in stock prices, but it is also true that the present outlook is not one that will support a completely negative attitude."

Or again, consider this classic item as reported by the Wall Street Journal. "If the 870–880 area in the DJI average cannot be overcome, I think the market will back away and test the lower part of the trading range around 840–850." No matter what happens it will be difficult to prove this interpretation wrong.

These quotes are from *daily* market letters. There are a few issued at less frequent intervals by brokers which contain original ideas based on sound research. But they are definitely in a minority. Significantly, these analysts don't recommend stocks to buy in every letter but only when a real value comes along or a UPB situation which the broker's corporate contacts has uncovered in its early stages. In contrast, most market letters recommend buying, buying, buying, even if they are issued every day. Then the impulsive investor who does buy is left high and dry.

If you think this is an exaggeration consider what the partner of a Wall Street house remarked not long ago—name withheld for obvious reasons. "A customer who followed all the firm's suggestions to the extent of 100 shares each would have needed $92 million in one year." He added, "we never told anybody to sell anything."

In short, market letters should be read as a source of ideas only, never as a guide to taking action. Seldom will their recommendations or timing fit the requirements of an individual's investment program. Even worse, such letters generally fail to see the forest for the trees. They are written from a short-term point of view whereas, the first requisite of successful investing is to manage your account from the long-pull point of view.

Actually, the seasoned broker doesn't want to give advice and does everything he can to avoid giving it. At best it's a thankless job. If he's right the customer takes the credit. If he's wrong, the customer, in due course, transfers his account to another firm. This is the main reason why some brokers experience such a rapid turn-over of accounts.

Unfortunately, the top partners of most firms have sold a bill of goods to the public about their willingness to supply unlimited quantities of free investment advice. "Send us your list of stocks"; they say, "and our research department will tell you what should be sold and what should be bought without any obligation on your part." This is an excellent way to get the names of prospective customers but there is some question as to its excellence as a source of sound and continuing investment advice.

True enough, the investment research department should be in a better position than the salesman to advise the customer. They have the time to sit down and review his portfolio in the light of his financial position and objectives (if he has any). But again there are serious drawbacks. In the first place the initial recommendations may be sound but they are rarely followed up and they are rarely part of a specific long-range program.

Furthermore, how unbiased is such an analysis? Can any one firm exhaustively analyze 10,000 stocks, any of which any customer may own? Another fact is that brokerage firms always seem to have a vested interest in promoting one stock or another. If they have been the underwriters for a certain corporation in the past, or if one of the senior partners is on the board of directors, the research department always seems partial to this particular stock regardless of its merit as an investment. It's only human nature.

Furthermore, very few men have the experience and "flair" needed to give consistently sound market advice. Such men command large salaries or, more likely, are in business on their own. But sometimes you can find a gifted analyst who spends his full time seeking UPB situations for the brokerage firms institutional clients. Once you locate such an individual cultivate him diligently. He may help you make a fortune.

Another occasional source of superior advice can be found among the advisory services. These fall into two categories: (1) The service that is essentially a promotional venture, designed to get new subscribers, and hence revenue, by hanging a carrot before prospective subscribers. And (2) the service that is dedicated to supplying a maximum of the minute facts and information on which every sound investment decisions must be based.

The difference between the two can be discovered by studying their advertisements and promotional literature. If a service promises to tell you the name of a stock that will double in price in a few months, beware. They are being intellectually dishonest. True, they may have recommended 25 stocks, one of which did double or triple in price in a short time, but this is not the route to a sound investment program. Subscribing to such a promotion oriented service can cost you peace-of-mind as well as loss of capital.

In the same category, but with better intentions, are a group of advisory services operated by market technicians who are trying their best to anticipate the intermediate market swings for their subscribers. These people mean well and will succeed at times, but they are trying to accomplish the impossible and in the end investors who follow their advice are bound to lose money. Most of these services are geared to some sort of gadget or technical market measurement which tells you when the market is about to go up—or down.

Finally, there are the investment advisory services that present a sound analysis of industry trends and individual stock developments. Every investor can benefit by subscribing to one or two of these services. The cost is nominal in relation to the value received. You should not pay any attention to their trend-of-the market predictions but pay a great deal of attention to their analysis of the outlook for the various industries and stocks within those industries. They may present facts which permit you to recognize a UPB stock even when they do not recognize the implications of their own research.

All told there are about 150 advisory services who get between $45 and $125 a year for their letters. How can so many survive when similar letters are available for free from brokers? The answer can be traced to the hundreds of thousands of misguided individuals who are out to make a fast dollar in the market. The advisory services give their customers what they want. In contrast, a broker—who also acts in a fiduciary capacity—must write with greater restraint.

The hapless get-rich-quick man certainly knows from bitter experience that *he* doesn't know the answers. He hears of other people who reportedly make killings when he regularly loses. Yet it looks so easy to make money trading. Possibly this service which submits proof that had you followed their advice between June 13, of last year, and June 27, of this year or some other carefully chosen dates, you would have increased your account by 27.75%; possibly they really do know whether the market is going up or down. After all, weren't they right at all the major turning points? (No, they weren't).

So he subscribes. Now if the service turns out to be wrong as often as right, does this discourage the customer? Not necessarily. Eventually, he may subscribe to a different service but seldom does he give up completely, at least not until he runs through his capital. Proof? The best source of leads for one service is a competitive list of ex-subscribers. This is one of the few businesses where competing firms are happy to trade their mailing lists of prospective subscribers.

The point is that the opinions of the service are influenced by the opinions of the subscribers, rather than vice-versa. In short, the subscriber gets what he wants. This means that the service will be bullish about 95% of the time. The remaining bearish letters will be inserted at intervals during a long bull trend. A reaction will be predicted and when it doesn't materialize the bullish position will be quickly reinstated. In this way, after a big decline—regardless of when it comes—the service that is on its toes can forevermore quote from a letter in which they predicted the bear trend with omnipotent accuracy. If the week before the collapse they actually advised buying with the sky the limit, they simply don't quote from *that* letter.

You say; "but the subscribers who got that last letter will know the service was wrong. Maybe they lost money. Won't they cancel their subscription?" Again the answer is no. Only a few will cancel or let their subscriptions lapse for this reason. Curiously, being wrong seldom hurts an advisory service. After all the customer is really calling the shots. He will be wrong when the service is. Hence, he will think the service is right at the time because he agrees with its interpretation. Usually months go by before it is really clear that the service was wrong. Meanwhile, the customer still agrees with his service.

It's not only *what* the market letter says but also how it's said. If written in a convincing and authoritative fashion and well promoted, advisory letters are a gold mine to their publishers. The well promoted letters may have from 5000 to 25,000 subscribers at $40 to $125 each. The profit margin may exceed 50% depending on whether the owners prefer to pay taxes or plow the profits back into more promotion. And regardless of the services' claim, advertising, direct mail and other promotional expenses will exceed the size of their investment research expenditures by a several-fold margin.

What about the letters that aren't authoritatively written, that aren't confidence inspiring and that don't even make sense? Strangely enough they still find their supporters. There seems to be more chronic optimists (or pessimistic bears) operating in the stock market than anywhere else. (They wouldn't be doing it if they were realistic. After all, as we have seen, the odds are better at Las Vegas when it comes to making *quick* profits.)

For many years we carried on a vastly amusing correspondence with Frederick Goldsmith, who attained fame of a sort by basing his predictions on the tips "they" (the insiders) were passing out via cartoons. The surprising thing was that Goldsmith was right more often than wrong and made a very good living. Some of his several hundred subscribers testified in his behalf in court and stated they had made a killing by following his recommendations.

During the period he wrote to us, the insiders (he claimed) were using cartoons in the New York Herald Tribune (why not the telephone?) to transmit inside information to each other. One cartoon shows a man who was so shocked by the price of his wife's new hat that he bit off the stem of his pipe. The bowl of the pipe was shown falling to the floor. Interpretation! The market would soon do likewise. (It promptly did sell off.) Goldsmith thought he was right because of the cartoons—but, he simply rationalized his decisions in a more bizarre manner than most of us do.

There are thousands of investment firms scattered about the countryside who specialize in selling mutual funds and unlisted securities. They also do a large investment counseling business. These firms cater almost exclusively to the unsophisticated investor. Their primary aim is to sell mutual funds because their profit is greatest on this type of business.

Their secondary aim is to sell unlisted stocks to their customers because their profit of 5% on unlisted issues is almost as great as the 6% or so they take on mutual funds. If you buy listed stocks through a majority of these firms you pay at least the usual stock exchange commission *plus* an added fee of perhaps 1 or 2% charged by the dealer.

This fee may also cover the firm's charge for their

investment counseling services. If so, let the customer beware. Any management fee that is tied to the activity in an account should be viewed skeptically. This is not a businesslike arrangement and will prove mutually unsatisfactory in the long run.

The fact that these firms may manage funds well up in the millions of dollars stands as a testimony to the trusting nature of the American public. Some of them even take a full power of attorney over their customer's accounts. However, few reputable investment counsel firms will ever accept a full power of attorney. A limited power will enable the manager to enter orders for the account but will leave the sole power to withdraw money where it belongs—in the hands of the client.

If you wish to buy a mutual fund, then by all means patronize your local investment dealer. But if you wish to own the listed shares of leading corporations as part of a sound long-range investment program, then take your business to a member firm of the New York Stock Exchange. This is not to suggest that an investment dealer will not do the best job he can for you with the securities he has to work with—he will. The standards of the National Association of Security Dealers are the highest and they see that their members adhere to them. Nevertheless, the proper function of a dealer is selling securities not managing portfolios.

If you feel that a professional investment manager can produce better results for you than you can for yourself, the person to go to is an investment counselor. For a moderate fee he will lift the entire load from your shoulders. (Fees usually range from ½ of 1% to 2% depending on the size of the account.) He does not have any stocks or bonds to sell you and does not have any incentive to "churn" your account. It's safe to say he is thinking—both consciously and subconsciously—only of your welfare.

If your account does well chances are his services will be retained. If not, chances are he will lose the account. This brings up one possible drawback. If your account has not performed well—perhaps the market has declined and all accounts have done rather poorly—there may be a tendency on the part of the counselor to "press." That is to take chances that would not ordinarily be taken in an effort to recoup past losses and hence, retain the account. But this is certainly only an outside possibility if you are dealing with a reputable counselor.

How does one go about locating the best counsel? Well the best isn't necessarily the biggest in this field. Many large investment counsel firms have produced very poor results for their clients and some individual counselors have produced outstanding results. Probably the most reliable recommendation is word of mouth. If any of your friends employ professional management ask them how they have fared. Or, ask a counselor you are considering for the names of several of his clients. He should be perfectly willing to give you their names (after first obtaining their consent). Naturally, he will direct you to those clients for whom he has been able to obtain the best results. Make allowance for this. But in any event if you do your part, you too may realize above average results.

When you decide to place your affairs in the hands of a professional, follow all of his recommendations promptly. Give him at least a period of two years to prove his worth.

The attitude of the client is quite as important as the ability of the counselor. The client who has a positive attitude, who has complete confidence in the counselor, who cheerfully encourages the counselor when the going is rough, who doesn't expect miracles—this client will achieve by far the best results.

CHAPTER 17

The Source of Reality

In the final analysis there can be only one ultimate source of information about any company—and that is the company itself. Why not go to the fountainhead for the information you need? If a company intrigues you, a good policy is to buy a small amount of the stock, then as a shareholder write to the company for the latest annual and interim financial statements, plus any other pertinent information that has been released to the press.

Study these reports carefully. They will usually raise as many questions as they answer. But sometimes these reports will contain all the information needed to recognize an authentic UPB situation. In which event you can proceed to take a larger position in the stock.

If, however, the published reports fail to answer vital questions then by all means go directly to a company spokesman. As a stockholder you have every right to question management and in a surprisingly large number of cases your questions will be answered honestly and completely. Of course, some topics will be out of bounds if the information revealed would provide you with advance information of such vital and major significance that it would obviously have an immediate influence on the price of the stock.

If you live near a large metropolitan area, chances are there will be several budding UPB candidates right in your own neighborhood. Your job is to find them and, as we have already mentioned, a good source of leads will be found among your local security analysts.

When in the process of appraising a likely candidate, make a personal visit to the head office and see for yourself. Depending on the size of the concern, you may be able to interview executives from the level of assistant to the president to a vice-president or even up to the president himself.

Some of the best investments we ever made originated in just this fashion. It was during a combination business-pleasure trip to Las Vegas, Nevada many years ago. Talks with the management of Nevada Power and Southwest Gas Corporation made it abundantly clear that both companies were destined to be UPB companies for many years to come. Without the personal visits, the conclusion would have carried much less weight.

A UPB was made possible not only by the extraordinary growth of the Las Vegas area, but also by a sudden consumer demand for year round air-conditioned homes. In addition, both companies advised us that the regulatory climate was favorable in Nevada—the reverse of the situation in California at that time.

The degree of confidence you have in your source of information should determine to some extent the degree of diversification in your portfolio. But in principle, if you can find 10 UPB stocks during their early stages *i.e.,* when they have risen only 50 to 100% above their pre-UPB days, then buy 100 shares of each rather than 1000 shares of only one of them.

Or, if you have complete confidence in stock A, almost complete confidence in stock B and a great deal of confidence in five other UPB stocks, then it would be logical to buy 300 shares of stock A, 200 of stock B, and 100 of each of the others.

An average size account should never invest in just one stock, rarely in only two or three and just as rarely in more than 10. In general, it is better to under than over diversify. Why? Because you should make every effort to know as much about each company you invest in as anyone in the country, including the top operating officials of the company itself. Now, there is a definite limit to how many separate situations you keep on top of to this extent. Certainly, it can not be more than 8 or 10, unless you have your own staff of security analysts.

In fact, at any one time there are not very many UPB companies around that are still in their early stages. The usual problem is finding a sufficient number to provide adequate diversification not deciding which ones should be eliminated.

And finally another reliable source of information about a company is its competitors. They will talk freely about problems that management may be reluctant to discuss at all. Competitors can provide an amazing quantity of accurate information about vital and presumably secret company trends, such as new products, etc.

CHAPTER 18

The Profits and Perils of Leverage

As soon as you find a UPB stock study its capital structure—it may have warrants outstanding which will enable you to make one dollar do the work of two or three in the common stock. But always remember leverage works both ways and it is much easier to lose half of your capital than it is to double it.

Warrants are considered to be the most speculative securities traded on the stock exchanges. In general this is true. Nevertheless, a few common stock warrants are blue-chip investment compared to a host of common stocks. Since warrants represent an option to buy a certain number of common shares at a certain price, a warrant is precisely as safe or risky as the common stock it is tied to. In effect, when buying warrants you buy the common shares minus any future dividends and with greater leverage per dollar expended because the warrants are usually lower priced than the common stock.

Warrants are created for a variety of reasons—none of which have any bearing on how to make money in them once they are listed on a stock exchange. In the first place, they are denied voting privileges, don't participate in earnings or dividends and often expire without fulfilling any apparently useful purpose. Ordinarily, warrants are employed as a "sweetener" to persuade the owners of one type of stock or bonds to agree to a recapitalization plan. Or, during periods of high interest rates warrants may be attached to new bond issues to facilitate their sale.

Fantastic claims are made about the profit potential in warrants. One advertisement tells how $500 invested in RKO warrants grew to $104,000 in four years. This is hindsight at its very best. For one thing, there were only a few warrants outstanding and they were traded over-the-counter. There was no interest in them and probably, not even $500 worth could have purchased anywhere near the low. If the low was $\frac{1}{64}$, a rise in, say $\frac{7}{8}$ represented the biggest portion of the final gain and may have taken place in a comparatively short space of time. When the RKO warrants finally expired they had no value whatever —not even one cent per warrant.

In recent years large profits apparently could also have been realized in the warrants issued by several highly speculative Canadian Oil and Mining stocks. Forget about these. An even larger number of these firms went broke and have never been heard from again. Nevertheless, such warrants have a peculiar attraction to some otherwise conservative investors. Such is the fascination of warrants that people who wouldn't touch the common stock of a company are willing to take a gamble in the warrants of the same company. Obviously, this is the height of irrationality.

Ideally, the only warrants to consider buying are those that have a perpetual option on the common at a fixed price *and are protected* against dilution.

Circumstances may arise which tend to dilute the

equity accruing to the warrants without affecting the prospects of the common shares. For instance, if the company distributes a large capital gain to shareholders or should a large stock dividend be declared, the warrants will be penalized accordingly if there is no provision in the corporate charter protecting them against dilution.

If a warrant expires in two or three years the premium it sells at (if any) will gradually narrow and if the common stock sells below the conversion price at the expiration date, the warrants will be worthless. This is not a theoretical danger but has actually happened many times in the past.

As a general rule, warrants are most attractive when the common stock sells slightly below the option price, or when they are priced at one fourth to one third of the price of the common stock. Warrants are the least attractive when the common sells well *above* the conversion price. Moreover, warrants may be *less attractive* than the common stock when the latter is selling *far below* the conversion price. The option feature represents a more or less fixed value; hence, as the common declines in price the warrants eventually reach a floor below which they sink with the greatest reluctance. At this level, the warrants become dormant and during the early stages of the next upswing the common stock may score the wider percentage gains.

To illustrate, when the Tri-Continental Corp. warrants which represent a perpetual option to buy 1.27 shares of common at $17.76/share, sold at 2⅛, the common sold at 6¼. A few years later the common had risen to 16¼ for a gain of 158%, whereas, the warrants rose only to 4 for a gain of 88.2%. However, by the time the common reached 34 the warrants had risen to 20¼. Appreciation in the warrants amounted to 412% compared to a gain of only 109% in the common stock.

Theoretically, warrants should be an ideal trading medium. Such is not the case. Warrants are just as difficult to trade in as common stocks—or more so. When warrants are the greatest bargain, commissions will be relatively high and the warrants may move in a narrow price range for years. Moreover, they may be difficult to buy and sell. If the market is thin, the spread between the bid and offer may represent 25% of the price, if the market is relatively active, thousands of warrants may be bid or offered ahead of you.

Should you become interested in investing in warrants but cannot find any issued by a UPB company, you should investigate those issued by investment trusts which will enable you to reduce the risk involved and provide some diversification.

This, of course, limits one's choice since at the present time there are only three well known warrants of investment companies being traded on the major exchanges. These are Atlas Corporation, Allegheny Corp. and the Tri warrants already mentioned. All of these issues are perpetual. While the first two are investment trusts, actually both managements are committed to special situations and there is no reliable correlation between the price action of either stock and the course of the market in general. On the other hand, Tri-Continental holds a broad cross section of American industry and the common stock closely adheres to the course of the market as a whole. The warrants, of course, do the same.

Here, then, is an ideal investment for an individual who

wishes to participate in the long-range future of this country, rather than assume the risks of investing in individual stocks or undertake the exhaustive research required to seek out UPB stocks. Although the Tri warrants will go down as well as up, they are *certain to participate in the next bull market and furthermore, are bound to gain* at least as much as the market averages. No one can buy any single stock and be *certain* of achieving an equally satisfactory performance, provided, of course, that stock prices stage substantial advances in the future as they have in the past.

Ordinarily, the amount of leverage in the warrant is a function of current market sentiment as well as other factors. Consider a warrant that represents the right to buy the common at 20. When the common stock sells at 10 the warrants may sell anywhere from 2 to 10. At 2 the leverage is large and the warrants are a bargain (if the common stock is also attractive). But at 10? Who conceivably would pay 10 for an option to buy the common at 20 when the common stock itself could be bought for 10?

Heaven above knows. But it does happen during periods of great speculative enthusiasm. And conversely, when warrants enjoy the greatest leverage for the least amount of money invested sentiment will be low and no one will want them.

CHAPTER 19

Securities to Avoid

Almost any company in any industry can become a potential Unique Profit Breakthrough situation. Who would have thought an ancient tobacco company would suddenly bloom into an authentic UPB stock? Or, a deadly dull bottle cap producer turn out to be one of the great growth stocks of our generation? So don't eliminate the staid old companies in mature industries from consideration. Lightning can strike anywhere, not just among the glamorous applied science companies, such as Control Data and Xerox. Moreover, the element of risk is usually much smaller in the former than in the latter type of stocks.

However, there are several classifications of stocks that should be avoided even in the face of favorable profit trends. These include a majority of foreign stocks, convertible securities, new issues and most low-priced stocks. Admittedly, this is an all-inclusive statement. It doesn't mean that many securities in each category aren't excellent investments from time to time. However, where the UPB concept obviously does not apply or where other disadvantages prevail, such as the difficulty of obtaining reliable information on many unlisted and foreign stocks,

156

you should eliminate such issues as likely UPB candidates.

The history, for example, of investment in foreign stocks and bonds is hardly one to cause rejoicing. Yet, in recent years, more and more foreign issues have achieved listing on our two major exchanges. The danger is that such a listing will be interpreted as an endorsement of the particular stock or bond by the exchange. To some extent such an interpretation is warranted but let the investor beware anyway. Moreover, the firsthand information needed is difficult to obtain when the head office is 5000 miles away.

Presumably, the government obligations of a foreign country are the safest investments that can be made in that country. The fact is, that at least 50% of all the foreign bonds that have ever been listed on the New York Stock Exchange have defaulted on their interest payments. Many sank to a fraction of their offering prices.

There is no school like experience and the lessons learned are not forgotten. One of our first investments was in a Bolivian tin company named Patino Mines. The stock was selling around 26 and paying between $3.00 and $4.00 annually. The company had a western hemisphere monopoly on tin and the mines were said to be inexhaustible. As is generally the case, the huge yield warned of trouble ahead. In due course, the Patino properties were nationalized following one of the periodic Bolivian revolutions and Patino stock lost 90% of its value. Fortunately we sold at 19 and the price of this lesson was a great bargain.

One of the favorite pronouncements of those who give

market advice is how you can have a bow with two strings by buying convertible securities. Here is a quote from a typical analysis published by a highly regarded firm.

"Issues of this type combine all the safety features of a top quality senior security and the appreciation characteristics of a common stock. The holder is thus protected against a continuation of the present price downtrend or an extended market rally in the months ahead."

Now this is a pernicious statement and nothing could be further from the truth. The fact is that convertible securities combine most of the disadvantages of both bonds and common stocks. The only time a case can be made for buying the convertible issue rather than the common stock is when the former is selling right at the conversion price *and is yielding more than the common stock*. This very rarely happens.

Despite their presumably defensive characteristics the fact is that if the common stock turns sour, so does the convertible issue. Sometimes, if the yield is large and secure it won't go down quite as fast, but this is hardly a sufficient reason for buying it in the first place. Meanwhile, when the outlook is promising, the convertible will usually sell several points above the conversion price which means two or three dollars may be required in the preferred or debenture to match the appreciation realized by one dollar invested in the common. Furthermore, the mere fact that the convertible shares are outstanding may tend to depress the common, which detracts from the attractiveness of both.

At times, a convertible issue will sell on an investment basis alone. That is to say, the price would probably be the same *without* the conversion feature. Under these conditions convertible preferreds and bonds can be attractive if you are interested in bonds, but only when a long period of easy money seems certain to lie ahead. That is, at a time when the bond prices seem likely to move up, yields down.

Unlike most new issues, convertible securities are usually the best buy—over the near-term—when initially offered. To insure the success of an offering, the company issuing the stock will offer a higher coupon than that paid by similar issues already outstanding. If the conversion price is not too high or if warrants are attached, such issues will immediately sell at a premium. In short, here is one of the stock market's few opportunities to garner short-term profits with relatively little risk.

There is a catch, of course. The larger the anticipated premium, the more difficult it will be to get a worthwhile position. The solution is to be on your broker's list of special customers. Otherwise, if the offering is "hot" you won't get any. If it is sour you will be able to buy (and urged to buy) all you want.

Rule: Except for unusually attractive new offerings, the best policy is to avoid convertible securities. *Never under any circumstances buy a convertible issue that is selling above its call price.*

The New Issue Illusion

Every so often a new issue comes along that everyone wants. A case in point was Comsat—which came out at 20 and soared to above 60 within a few weeks. Usually such a well publicized event sets off a scramble for *any* new issue. At such times illusion takes over completely. But first a look beneath the surface of the new issue market.

The machinery needed to underwrite and then market a new issue is elaborate, the rewards, if successful, are great and the risk, if not successful, may be even greater. For this reason a syndicate of from 10 to 100 firms is usually formed to spread the risk and also to put more salesmen to work on the selling job. The underwriters profit for selling the new issue will range from about 5% for the issue of a large corporation with the best credit rating to 20% for a speculative issue. This means that if the public subscribes $1 million for a new issue of stock the corporation raising the money will realize between $800,000 and $950,000.

So far so good, but from the standpoint of the individual investor who is also intent upon his own welfare as well as the welfare of the corporation, the underwriter, and his salesmen, there is another side to the coin. The trouble stems from two conditions. First, the commission paid to the salesman (a name which is variously disguised as registered representative, account executive or customer's man) is generally four or five times greater than for a comparable transaction in a listed stock.

It stands to reason that the salesman will try four or five times as hard to sell you a new offering as he will the listed issue you intended to buy all along. Here, if anywhere, let the buyer beware.

If you choose to ignore the advice offered in this chapter and go ahead and buy a new issue, be sure to read and understand thoroughly every word in the offering prospectus—especially, if the new issue totals less than

$300,000. Such an offering can often be marketed without first registering it with the SEC. The danger of fraud is great unless you personally are acquainted with the character of the promoters.

Even with larger issues, which must be registered with the SEC, you can't be too careful. Remember, the SEC doesn't pass on the merits of any issue. But, it does do its best to disbar those issues where the prospectus contains false statements or omits vital information. Moreover, if the prospectus is not misleading the SEC is helpless to proceed regardless of how unfavorable the provisions of the offering are for the buyer.

So here are the points to watch for. How much commission does the underwriter get? How much extra stock have the promoters pigeonholed for themselves and at what price? What extra expenses are involved? Just how sound does the new venture appear to be? Or, if it is a privately held, going operation is there a UPB possibility? View the most recent earnings figures with reservation. Usually new issues are marketed at precisely the time that earnings are at a temporary peak.

Each year the SEC holds up numerous new issues —sometimes indefinitely—until the provisions of the Securities Act of 1933 are fulfilled. In a typical recent case promoters proposed to raise $1,750,000 through an offering of convertible debentures. Selling commissions and expenses totaled $312,500 or about 18% of the capital to be raised. It should be pointed out that this is not unusually high for a speculative venture. However, the principals were virtually without assets of any kind, there was no firm commitment by underwriters as individuals for any part of the offering. Gross profits were projected at over $500,000 based on a survey that had never been made. The business experience of the officers and directors was misrepresented. And as a clincher, the registration statement failed to disclose that *all* of the common equity in the corporation was to be sold to the officers and directors for an amount not in excess of $2,500! *Not in excess of $2,500*. This was adding insult to injury. Probably the promoters were planning to acquire all of the common stock for one dollar.

If you are interested in the sociological aspects of marketing new issues, the posturings of some brokers should prove enlightening. If the new stock is "sticky" i.e., astute investors and institutions won't touch it, you may receive a phone call from some enterprising customer's man. That is, if he is doing his job, which is to sell his firm's securities. Usually he will proceed to give you a glowing picture of the opportunities awaiting the purchaser of 100 shares of the rejuvenated Threadbare Carpet Company. The company may have paid dividends only twice in the past 30 years but new management has aggressively diversified into cosmetics, house trailers, uranium and inevitably—oil exploration. Earnings should, by a conservative estimate, double this year. If this spiel sounds familiar—enough said. In the stock market high-pressure selling spells danger.

Usually, the clinching argument is that you can buy the stock being offered *without paying any commission*. Strictly speaking this is true. But the company or selling stockholders offering the stock will be paying from 5 to 20 times the usual commission and you are buying their stock. The salesman will be receiving four or five times the usual commission for himself. Furthermore, about nine times out of ten, if you do want to buy this particular stock you can simply wait until a few weeks after the underwriters close their books and buy it at a substantial discount from the offering price, thereby, saving several commissions for yourself.

To facilitate such offerings investment bankers employ an ingenious device known as "stabilizing." If a stock is being offered at $50 per share, then the free market price is not allowed to fall below this price until the offering has been all absorbed by the public. Except in a runaway bull market, stabilization will be necessary. After all, if 100,000 or 500,000 new shares are being offered, the most elementary reasoning will conclude that supply may exceed demand for sometime to come—and it usually does.

When the syndicate is doing a really first-rate job they will—if it can be done cheaply—actively run the price of the stock up a point or so, thereby creating the impression that "good" buying is going on despite the offering—a practice which has been found to effectively lower the sales resistance of the customers. A classic example was afforded by a huge secondary offering of Olin-Mathieson Corporation common stock. Prior to this offering a series of sensational developments had been announced by Olin management. First, came the dramatic announcement that the Squibb division had made progress in developing a treatment for certain types of cancer. A tremendous speculative demand pushed the stock from 50 to 58. A month later the company announced that a new $36-million plant was under construction to produce revolutionary high energy fuels based on the glamor metal—boron. The possibilities were said to be enormous and Olin promptly pushed to a new high above 60 on even greater volume of trading.

Thus, the stage was set for parties unknown to make a secondary distribution of 165,000 shares at 60½. As soon as the news was released, Olin sold off to 59 and a fraction only to rally strongly back to 60½ where the price normally would be pegged until the 165,000 shares had been distributed. But at this juncture "they"—presumably the syndicate—put the stock up to 61½ and as a result, the 165,000 shares went "out the window." Thereafter, the stock plummeted more than 20 points without a rally of any consequence and this was the last time Olin sold above 60 for many years. According to figures published by the SEC, it is not uncommon for thousands of stabilizing operations to be carried out in the course of a year.

Here is a rule of thumb which will be unpopular with investment bankers but which may save you—as an individual investor—a lot of money. If a large block of stock being offered to the public is "sticky," or if for any other reason the syndicate needs to stabilize the price, sell out at once. The chances are great that the shares will sink to lower levels. The longer the underwriters have to stabilize the market for the stock, the more imperative it is to sell the stock. Needless to say, you should never buy any shares on such an offering.

You may have had a salesman tell you that you can't turn around and sell a new issue while the market is being "stabilized." This is simply not true. Obviously, the underwriters, who may be buying to stabilize the price at the very time their salesmen are selling, don't want to buy any more shares than necessary. Nor do they like to see short sales being made for the same reason. Salesmen who encourage their customers to take this sort of action will soon be seeking a new connection. Nevertheless, should your broker refuse to execute such orders for you, you can be certain some other broker who is not a member of the underwriting group will execute the order with pleasure.

The mathematical odds against new issues are overwhelming—especially if the new issues are also low-priced. For example, we recently surveyed at random 60 stock issues in the $1 to $3 range which came out in 1963. Despite the fact that the market has been rising since then, currently, only six of the 60 are selling at or above the offering price, 54 below it. For 37 of the 54 there was no market at all. And the same dismal story was true 10 years ago and will be true 10 years from now. Thus, according to a study made by Financial World Magazine, in 1956, 140 low priced issues were offered to the public. By February, 1958, 22 were selling above the original offering price, seven were unchanged while the remainder were quoted below the offering price—often as much as 80 or 90%. Here again, there was no market at all for more than half (73) of the issues. On the other hand, only six of the 140 stocks had more than doubled in price. Enough said. Anyone who risks hard-earned money in this manner deserves to lose it—and will.

Over-the-Counter Stocks

The case for avoiding over-the-counter stocks is not nearly as strong as for avoiding convertible bonds, preferreds, or new and secondary offerings—very often UPB diamonds can be found among unlisted stocks. All of the great growth stocks were traded on the OTC market before graduating to an exchange. Nevertheless, there are some 35,000 stocks traded OTC and the line must be drawn somewhere. This is another good place to draw it.

In the first place, it is usually more difficult to get reliable information on unlisted stocks. Furthermore, the information that is available is not always accurate. Unfortunately, dealers in unlisted stocks usually have more to gain (and more risk of loss) than firms dealing in listed securities. The dealer in O.T.C. stocks buys and sells for his own account so he tries to buy low and sell high. In contrast, the broker in listed stocks simply acts as an intermediary between buyer and seller for a fixed fee which is standardized by the stock exchanges.

And while the O.T.C. market has improved it still has room for additional improvement. For example, here is a recent series of orders placed in a well known O.T.C. stock. Although around 1.5 million shares were outstanding, the market—like that for most unlisted issues—was thin. The stock was quoted at 54½ bid 55½ offered. A return order was immediately entered to sell 100 shares at 54½. Nothing happened. The broker got a new quote which was now 53½ bid 54½ offered. A new order was immediately entered at 53½ and again nothing happened. In the end the stock was sold at 51½. A strenuous effort is being made by dealers in unlisted stocks to ensure firm bids and offers, but the very nature of this market impairs its liquidity.

Another drawback to owning unlisted stocks is that you either can't borrow at all on them, or you can borrow less than on a listed stock in the same price range. Why?

Well, moneylenders are a pretty shrewd lot and this fact illustrates more clearly than words that they don't think unlisted stocks represent as safe collateral as listed stocks.

The preceding comments do not apply to two industries—banks and insurance companies—which are traded over the counter. Ordinarily the market for these issues is as active and broad as for listed stocks. And often UPB candidates will be found in these industries. Banks and insurance companies prefer not to have their shares listed on a national stock exchange because the prices at which they are quoted are more readily available. The theory is that their depositors or policyholders would lose confidence in the enterprise if they saw the price declining and thus, they are less likely to become aware of such a development if the shares are unlisted. However, this prejudice seems likely to weaken now that a major bank —Chase Manhattan—has been listed on the New York Stock Exchange.

Avoid Secondhand Buying

Assume that the long-term outlook for the aircraft industry appears superior to that of most industries, which happens to be the case as this is written. Sooner or later these stocks will become fashionable with investors and speculators alike and will start moving up on heavy volume. One or two companies will be real UPB situations and so will move up most, yet many investors will be attracted to those issues that are "behind" the group or behind the market. This is a mistake. If Boeing or General Dynamics are the stocks with the most dynamic UPB potential, buy both of them and avoid the marginal firms that are lagging behind the parade. These stocks will always appear to be cheaper but they seldom are in the long run.

Similarly, assume the outlook for stock "A" is outstanding, the company has made a valid UPB and so the shares are moving up rapidly. Stock "B" owns a large block of stock "A." Unless the outlook for stock "B" is fully as good as the prospects for stock "A" (without considering its block of stock A) don't buy stock B in the hope that these hidden values will eventually be reflected in a higher price for the stock. Buy Stock "A" directly.

Let's substitute some names for "A" and "B." Book-of-the-Month Club owns 273,742 shares of Grosset & Dunlap—a leading publisher of paperback, juvenile and other books. If, after careful investigation, you are convinced that Grosset & Dunlap qualifies as an authentic UPB situation because of their radical new marketing policies or the vastly increasing educational expenditures, then buy G & D, not Book-of-the-Month Club.

Companies Worth More Dead Than Alive

Security analysts like to dig around in musty corners and come up with lists of stocks they advocate buying because the working capital per share is greater than the market price. Occasionally this approach will lead you to an authentic UPB company. Or, sometimes liquidation will occur at a price well above the market, but generally the company's management will bitterly fight any move calculated to abolish their jobs. Only a handful out of hundreds of the "worth more dead than alive" companies are ever liquidated to the resulting advantage of the stockholders.

In general, these companies have poor growth records and are operating in retrogressive industries. Good stocks sell at wide premiums over net working capital per share. Thus, General Electric with working capital of only $12 per share sells near 100. Dow Chemical's working capital amounts to around $8 per share, yet Dow sells for 10 times that figure while IBM with working capital of only $23 per share sells for 20 times as much.

Furthermore, large working capital is due usually to large inventories (which the company may have trouble selling at cost). Retail concerns such as Montgomery Ward will usually have a relatively large working capital because of the huge inventories required to operate their retail stores and mail-order business. Similarly liquor company stocks often sell below net working capital because of the tremendous inventory of aging whiskey that is carried on the books as a current asset.

So unusually large net working capital *alone* should not be a determining factor in stock selection unless management is using the assets to create a UPB situation.

When you or your advisor's research has unearthed a promising UPB stock, the mechanics of accumulating your position can make or cost you a sizable sum depending on your knowledge of how to enter orders under varying market conditions.

CHAPTER 20

Money-Making Pointers

The morning after an especially momentous news event the market will open sharply higher—or lower. Many stocks can't be opened for an hour or longer and then only at wide changes from the previous close. If the news is bullish—say a Cuban or a Chinese dictator has a heart attack—orders will be entered to buy, perhaps 20,000 or more shares of, say, U. S. Steel. Meanwhile, most sell orders have been cancelled.

The specialist in steel must proceed to round up enough sellers to supply 20,000 shares. Usually the specialist and other floor traders will supply part of the stock and also sell some short to help supply the demand. The remainder of the 20,000 shares will be supplied by individuals or institutions who, however, are only willing to sell at a considerably higher price than the previous close. If steel closed at 55, the sellers may be asking from 56 to 65 for their stock. If 20,000 shares are available at prices ranging from 56 to 58½, then the Board of Govenors of the stock exchange will be consulted and will set a fair price for the sale of the 20,000 shares—in this case $58.50 per share.

If another momentous event is construed by the majority as being bearish, orders to sell will flood the floor of the exchange and stocks will open down several points. More often than not the opening price will mark the low in this instance—or, if the delayed opening is on the upside the high for a stock over the near-term at least. Two rules apply here. Never buy with the crowd on a delayed upside opening. Never sell on a delayed downside opening. On the other hand, if you have been planning to sell or buy, as the case may be, a delayed opening presents an ideal opportunity to effect your transaction. Of course, you will buy if sellers predominate and sell only if buyers predominate. Under these conditions always enter market orders.

Frequently, important news will be released between the time the New York Stock Exchange closes and the close of the Pacific Coast Stock Exchange. If the news is bullish, eager traders will promptly buy stocks on the coast and prices will close there above their closing prices in New York. Next day the market in New York will open *lower* than the close on the Pacific Coast Exchange. The rule here: "If you wish to buy wait a few days. If you wish to sell, sell on the coast the day the news is released—providing, of course, your stock is traded on that exchange."

Stop Loss Orders

Stop loss orders have no place at all in the strategy employed by investors, and since traders are going to lose anyway it doesn't much matter how they do it; with or without stop loss orders the final outcome will be the same.

The net result of using stop orders is about the same as arbitrarily selling out if a stock declines 10%. Such orders are yet another mechanical substitute for judgment. An investor who buys a stock at 50 and then enters a stop loss order to sell at 45 in an effort to prevent being locked into a loss, is falling into the trap that causes investors to unknowingly wind up as speculators. *Anyone who uses stop orders is a trader pure and simple.*

Clearly, if a stock is purchased at 50 and the buyer is willing to sell it in a few days merely because the market is now quoted at 45, then the stock should never have been bought in the first place. Moreover, the fact that we hope the stop order will *not* be executed reveals the futility of entering it in the first place.

Of course, it may also transpire that conditions affecting a stock have changed shortly after its purchase, or it may become apparent that poor judgment had been used in making the original purchase. If the stock was bought at 50 and is quoted at 48, there is often a tendency to enter a stop loss order at, say, 44 and hope for the best. Don't do it. If you think you have made a mistake sell out at once. But be certain that the *poor price action alone* is not the cause of your reappraisal. In fact, the safest policy is not to check the price of a stock at all until at least six weeks have elapsed after its purchase.

Entering Orders

Should you enter market or limit orders? If there is any clear-cut answer to this question, we don't know what it is. Sometimes if you enter market orders you will pay a point or one-half point more than the person who buys the stock 5 minutes later. On the other hand, if you enter a limit order to sell, your order won't be executed and the market proceeds to tumble—at least this is the way it seems to work out more often than not. Or again, if you enter an order to buy at 40, the stock will trade at 40 then move right up to 43 *without filling your buy order*—other orders were ahead of you.

If entering limit orders appeals to you and you are patient enough to wait your chance and risk missing the market altogether, then it is usually advantageous to enter buy orders ⅛ point above a round number and sell orders ⅛ below the nearest round number. This will often be the margin that will enable your order to be filled in an actively traded stock.

You can also usually enter "not held" orders which allows the floor broker to use his best judgment when executing the order. He may wait three or four hours before filling the order or even a day or two—if in his judgment it will be to the customer's advantage to do so. Obviously, his judgment may turn out to be wrong. But in the long run your executions will be better than if you enter orders "at the market," or limit them to a fixed price. This method of entering orders is almost mandatory when fairly large blocks of stock are involved.

A few years ago a floor broker received an order to sell 1500 shares of a rather inactive stock. The market was bid 33⅛, offered at 33¾; the size: 100 shares bid, 100 shares offered. During the day the broker managed to sell the entire 1500 shares at 33⅝, which was the high for the day and ever since—the stock now sells around 10. If the order had been entered at a limit price, say 34, the seller would not have gotten off even 100 shares.

Hedging Your Bets

Occasionally, an investor (who is really interested in trading, although he may not admit it), will turn in desperation to the hedged position. After losing money in a rising market as well as losing money in a declining market, he hits upon a fool proof solution. Eureka! *Why not be both long and short at the same time?*

This sounds sensible but it isn't. Only the most gifted stock exchange member has ever made money consistently in this way. Such a plan combines the difficulties of trading and short-selling.

There is still another form of hedging that has appeal in some situations. At times there will be considerable doubt in your mind as to the correct action to take. At these times you may wish to complete only *part* of the contemplated action. For instance, you think you should sell your commitment in a UPB stock which is meeting stronger competition but there is still considerable doubt in your mind. After all the stock looks "high" but is still rising. In this situation why not sell one-quarter or one-half of your holding? Or, you have decided to buy a potential UPB stock, but have not completed your research, yet the market and the stock are moving up strongly. Why not buy one quarter or one third of your contemplated purchase now, the remainder when and if your investigation confirms the validity of the UPB for this company?

At this point many investors will reply: Either a stock should be held or it should be sold. Strictly speaking this is correct—at least hindsight will indicate so. But in this business all of the facts can seldom be known; the picture is not always 100% clear. Success, as we have seen, is a relative matter so there is no reason why it isn't good policy to hedge until the missing facts upon which a firm decision can be made are available.

And more important, the person who hedges is less

likely to suffer psychologically. If he sells out his entire position only to see the stock he sold soar higher and higher, his disappointment may well adversely influence his subsequent attitude and judgment for months or years. Similarly, if he fails to sell until a stock declines to a fraction of its earlier high, his tendency will be to sell too soon when a new UPB campaign gets underway.

Cause and Effect in the Stock Market

One of the most common errors everyone makes is to assign the wrong causes to a given effect. For instance, a person recovers from a common cold after taking bicarbonate of soda, eating oranges, taking vitamin C, whiskey or some other remedy being used at the time of his recovery. He is convinced that his pet remedy caused his recovery, yet exhaustive research has conclusively proved that *nothing* cures a cold. It must run its course, at least this is true in the mid-1960's.

Seldom can the true causes ever be determined for any of the developments or events that affect our lives. Usually a multitude of causes will be contributing to the effect, only a few of which are known to the observer. In retrospect, the most familiar or the most logical causes will be chosen in an effort to explain why an event took place. More often than not such rationalizations will be wrong.

This is especially true in the stock market where the emotions of thousands of individuals may be influencing the price trend of a single stock. To try to anticipate what effect a known influence will have on stock prices is a matter of guesswork, pure and simple. True enough, *unexpected* news that is clearly bearish will usually cause a temporary price decline, and unexpected good news a temporary price bulge. But there are a great many exceptions to this rule and the exceptions can prove painfully costly to the investor who acts on the news.

The fact is, the same piece of news may cause prices to rise one time and decline the next. Which result transpires depends on a multitude of factors, mostly unknown. Therefore, if the market declines on a piece of good news, the news is said to have already been discounted. Or, possibly, the explanation is that the technical condition of the market is weak and it's ripe for a decline anyway. Obviously this is true but as a cause it's meaningless.

Or again, if you buy a stock and it moves up, you will naturally conclude that the reason which prompted you to buy was the principal cause of the rise. Perhaps you bought the stock because the market price was lower than the company's net working capital per share, or because the yield was a liberal 7%, or possibly, because the company held a block of stock in another company which was valued at only a fraction of its true worth. If the stock does go up, more than likely other and often unknown reasons cause it. The next time you make a similar decision to buy, the stock will probably decline.

We can recall a very thorough and competent analysis of Northern Pacific Railroad, issued by a prominent security analyst in 1949. His conclusion: "Nipper" was drastically undervalued. Shortly thereafter, oil was discovered in the Williston Basin where NP had—and still has—large holdings of land. Undoubtedly, this analyst attributed the ensuing spectacular rise to the deep undervaluation that existed in 1949 rather than to the speculative appeal of the oil discovery.

This whole problem of undervalued and overvalued is indeed, a fascinating one. No one ever agrees on a definition for these terms so we will coin one. An undervalued stock is one that subsequently advances in price. An overvalued stock one that soon declines.

The fact that the stock market very often behaves in a way contrary to what one might anticipate based on common sense, had led to the "Theory of Contrary Opinion." Many analysts will attempt to forecast the future trend of the market by "coppering" majority opinion. Like most forecasting gadgets this one is right just often enough to make the theory appear plausible. The problem is to determine whether majority opinion is really bullish or bearish at any given time. This can be done *reliably* only *after* the turning point has been passed and even then difficulties are encountered.

Theory has it that after the market has declined for some time "everyone" becomes bearish and confidently looks for still lower prices. But since bearishness has become universal, it means everyone has already sold all the stocks they are willing to part with. Hence, whether the news is good or bad it will be greeted as a reason to buy rather than sell. The market will then soar much to everyone's surprise. But what about those individuals who *bought* all the stock that was being sold on the decline? Mightn't they decide to sell at the time that everyone was confidently looking for still lower prices? The answer—at times—is yes. Anyone who held or bought stocks during 1930, 1931, 1937, 1946 or early 1962 will vouch for the accuracy of this statement.

Proponents of the contrary approach cite such times as the outbreak of World War II in 1939, to support their theory. In August stock prices were near their lows for the year and everyone expected the market would crash if war broke out. Instead prices skyrocketed. So obviously, not everyone was bearish on the outbreak of war. Very well then. Let's refine the theory. The public or the majority was bearish (aren't they always wrong?) and that charmed minority who are always right were bullish. By now you're playing with deuces wild and who can refute this argument?

But what about the events that took place nine months later, in May, 1940? When Hitler invaded France and Belgium the market collapsed overnight and prices plummeted far below their lows of 1939. If war breaks out tomorrow will the market go up or down? Who knows? It all depends. One thing we do know. Trying to guess what "the market will do" is a futile, costly, time-wasting pastime.

Minimizing Taxes

No one likes taxes. But the special hostility of investors towards the capital gains tax seems overdone. Even those who feel a tax on capital gains is wrong in principle and purely a political expedient, should at the same time, be realistic and appreciate that the capital gains tax is a blessing in disguise. It has *made and saved* more money for investors than it will ever *take* from them. Why? Simply because the long-term trend of stock prices has been up and this tax has effectively prevented millions of investors from selling their good stocks too soon. It encourages people to sell stocks held at a loss and hold stocks held at a profit—which is usually correct policy.

Consider a high tax bracket man who holds Xerox

Corp. (or any other UPB stock) at an adjusted cost of one dollar a share. When the stock reached 2 or 3 or 4, chances are he would have sold out but for the tax liability. Would he have held the stock all the way to 50 or to 100 or to 200? Not one person in a hundred would. Yet, this is precisely the way to build a fortune. Patience is an investor's greatest attribute and the tax on capital gains has created many patient investors.

In the final quarter of each year millions of shares of stock are sold by alert investors who are striving to reduce their tax burden. This is a commendable goal but far too often the largest part of these sales don't accomplish what they set out to.

For one thing, most of us are inclined to sell only when it will reduce rather than increase our tax load. Nevertheless, and contrary to popular belief, selling to establish a profit often can more effectively lower taxes than selling to establish a loss. Moreover, one simple truism is often overlooked. Namely, whatever the reason, selling is best done when prices are high rather than low.

Clearly, the lower the tax bracket the smaller the savings that can be realized by taking losses. Yet, too many investors automatically register losses without carefully weighing the disadvantages as well as the theoretical advantages.

An investor who sells a stock solely to establish a loss would—unless he is in the top tax bracket—be better off simply to hold the stock. If the outlook for the stock is sound it will probably recover when tax selling subsides. The fact is, that the market often records its low for the year in the late fall when tax selling reaches a peak. The investor who sells and holds the cash may suffer a loss in equity far in excess of the tax saving. Or, if this demoralizing fate is to be avoided, it is necessary to immediately reinvest in another stock which will recover in price as much as the one sold and will also fit into the investor's investment program equally well. This is a maneuver that is easier to contemplate than to accomplish.

Suppose you hold a stock at a 10-point loss. Assuming you earn $12,000 and file a joint return, by establishing the loss you can reduce your tax on ordinary income by $260. This sounds fine. But if you sell the stock at 50, say, and replace it with a similarly situated issue also selling at 50, expenses would amount to about $90.

Moreover, when buying and selling some price concession usually must be made by the person initiating the trades. Let us estimate that this less obvious "attrition" averages about ¾ of a point. That means the theoretical $260 saving is cut to $95 *or less than a one-point recovery in the stock sold.*

But what if you decide to take the loss and retain your original position? This procedure also has disadvantages. Since the shares sold cannot be repurchased within 30 days (if the loss is to be used) you can (1) buy an equivalent number of shares 31 days before selling or (2) repurchase the stock 30 days after the sale was made. The first alternative requires additional capital and is a highly speculative undertaking. After all, if the stock continues to decline the loss will be doubled. In the second alternative, the stock may rise during the 30-day interval by a greater margin than the tax saving realized. Not only can you suffer a demoralizing loss but your entire investment program may be upset by losing the position.

One general rule covers all tax problems. Stocks should be bought and sold on the basis of their future profit potential and only secondarily in an effort to reduce tax liability.

Supply and Support Levels

Stock charts should seldom be used as an aid to selecting stocks but they are helpful as an aid to buying and selling at the best possible price. Anyone who has studied stock charts for a long period of time cannot fail to notice the tendency for a stock to hesitate or consolidate a move at a supply or support level. You can't "trade" on these recurring patterns (as differentiated from chart formations) because the attrition against the trader is so overwhelming. But paying attention to this simple concept will often help in determining at what general price level long-term positions should be taken or closed out.

As the name suggests a supply level is the price at which a large number of shares are likely to be offered. A support level is the price at which a large number of buy orders are likely to materialize. How can these levels be recognized?

Assume a stock has risen 200 or 300% over a period of years and then fluctuates between 60 and 64, say, for several months. Then a piece of adverse news comes along or the market as a whole declines and the stock plunges to 52 in a matter of days. 60–62 now becomes a supply area. Why? Hundreds of thousands of shares have been traded at prices ranging between 60 and 64. A large percentage of these shares may have been bought by individuals who hope to make a quick profit—or, in other words, who haven't any sound reason for buying at all.

Many of these individuals may not even know what business the company is engaged in. These shares are said to be in "weak hands."

These traders watch the stock start down and are not especially upset when it reacts to 58, but as the decline continues to 56, 54, and then 52, their misgivings rapidly mount. The most emotional individuals and those holding the stock on maximum margin may sell in disgust or panic around 52. The others mentally say to themselves; "if it ever gets back to 60, 62 or as the case may be, 64 they can have it. All I want is to get out even."

Bargain hunters and long-pull investors will now come into the market and the stock will rally to 60–62 at which point the rally runs into a large supply of stock and the advance bogs down.

Should conditions affecting this company be particularly adverse the rebound might carry back only to the 55–57 area before a continuation of the decline sets in. On the other hand, if the outlook for earnings and the long-range prospects are bright, the stock might simply hesitate for several days or weeks at the 60–62 barrier before surging through the overhead supply and scoring a new high.

Support levels act in the same way as supply levels only in reverse. If a stock trades for many months in a narrow range with a low of 20 and high of 24, then breaks out on the upside to 28, the 22–24 area will be one of strong support for a number of reasons. For one thing, the long interval spent in a narrow range always tries the patience of speculators (who are looking for fast action) and, unfortunately it also tries the patience of too many investors.

When the speculator who sells out at 23, 24, or 25 sees his long-dormant stock soar through the old highs to 28, or 30 he figures the big move he was waiting for is now underway and plans to reinstate his position on the first reaction back to the price at which he sold out. Understandingly enough, very few people are willing to rebuy a stock at a higher price than they received for the same stock only a short time before. Meanwhile, traders who didn't have a position in the stock are attracted by the sudden move and they too, await a reaction to buy in.

Now assume this stock does back and fill in the 26–30 area (those who hope to buy at 24 won't get the chance), and then a new advance gets underway which carries the stock up to 40. The 28–30 level will now become the new support zone and reactions will tend to run their course somewhere between 40 and 30.

Stock market analysts are fond of referring to the market's position as being technically strong (or weak) without defining these terms. Presumably the technical position is strong if there are more potential buyers than sellers at a given price and vice versa. These are hazardous predictions to make, since circumstances can arise overnight which convert prospective sellers into buyers or discourage prospective buyers into leaving their cash in the bank.

Nevertheless, some generalizations will prove to be right more often than wrong. Thus, in the first example discussed above the technical position of the stock was weak after a long rise and then several months spent in a trading range without any further upside progress. Those who bought during this interval will be discouraged by the lack of upside activity (in the case of investors the long rise and high prices may discourage purchases). On the other hand, the longer the stock holds in the trading range individuals who bought the stock at lower prices will be more and more inclined to take their profit. Some experts refer to this as an area of distribution or even as a "distributive top" for the interest of those who collect redundant phrases.

But should the stock proceed to break out on the upside—scoring an all-time high—the technical position is strong and probably will remain so for some time. When a stock is "in the clear" all shareholders, of course, have paper profits. No one is waiting to "get out even." Hence, until such time as the fundamentals affecting the company begin to deteriorate the strong holders have no incentive to sell. One principle should be stressed again and again. If the UPB concept continues to be valid *never* sell a stock that is chalking up new highs.

A final thought on volume of trading. In speculative stocks it will be negligible at a bottom and will reach climactic proportions at a top. In contrast, volume of trading in the blue chips will be greatest at a bottom and least at a top (in relationship to the total volume for all stocks). The reason for this divergent pattern is plain. True investors—which is to say institutional investors and the like—buy value and values are usually greatest when prices are low. In contrast, those seeking speculative profits, which is to say the public, are attracted to stocks that are on the move, in the hope that they will go a few points higher.

CHAPTER 21

What To Do About Inflation

There are two kinds of inflation—price inflation and monetary or credit inflation. They may or may not occur simultaneously. Price inflation may be aggravated by monetary inflation but it can and often does occur when monetary *deflation* is taking place. In this situation the demand for goods and commodities exceeds the supply even at a time when inflationary purchasing media is on the decline.

Monetary inflation takes place when the money supply is being increased at a rate faster than needed to finance the production and distribution of goods. Assume for instance, that a manufacturer of mouse traps borrows $50,000 from a bank to finance the production of a new model. The bank *creates* a deposit of $50,000 *that did not previously exist*. Part of this money is spent for material, wages, etc. and, since the $50,000 represents newly created money it is for a time inflationary, but as soon as the mouse traps are sold and the $50,000 loan is paid off no monetary inflation has taken place because the credit was all used to produce, sell and distribute goods (the same would be true if a service had been sold rather than mouse traps).

Now, assume this manufacturer needed only $50,000

to finance his manufacturing and selling costs but, from his study of the economy, he anticipated a price increase in the cost of the steel wire used in his traps. Instead of borrowing $50,000 he decided to borrow $75,000 and buy an additional $25,000 worth of steel wire in anticipation of selling it for a higher price later on. Since this $25,000 was not used for productive purposes, it is inflationary.

Inflationary purchasing media can be created in many ways and it can be liquidated in many ways. One of the best ways to create it is to build aircraft, missiles and tanks using borrowed money that will never be paid back. The armaments are soon destroyed or become obsolete while the debt remains.

Another way is through deficit financing. The point to remember is that when monetary inflation is taking place more money is available to flow into securities and help fuel higher prices. When monetary deflation is taking place less money is available for the stock market and usually this situation will cause a net flow of money *out* of the securities markets which means, of course, that most stocks will decline. The services mentioned in an earlier chapter which analyze the banking statistics all publish valuable measurements of the degree and trend of monetary inflation. The American Institute for Economic Research—a nonprofit organization—also publishes an index of inflation.

There is a rather reliable relationship between monetary inflation or deflation and the trend of stock prices. The stock market usually turns up several months or longer after the inflationary portion of the money supply begins to increase. It turns down several months, or longer, after the inflationary portion of the money supply begins to decrease.

Drastic monetary inflation has been a characteristic of all wars since money first was used as a medium of exchange. Between 1915 and 1919 inflationary purchasing media increased dramatically and so did stock prices. By 1921 practically all of this monetary inflation had been liquidated and so had practically all of the rise in stock prices.

Between 1924 and early 1929 another period of monetary inflation was witnessed. The Federal Reserve System followed an easy money policy which supplied the purchasing power for speculation in real estate and stocks. Yet during this period of monetary inflation the prices of commodities and goods were actually declining. This, then, was a period of monetary inflation and price deflation (except in the stock market).

Again between 1933 and 1936 a period of credit inflation financed a bull market in stocks. Without question, the average stock was more overvalued in 1936–37 than at any other time in the history of the stock market. The reason: Capital flowed into stocks rather than into new capital ventures. The bull market was not founded on corporate prosperity but solely on monetary inflation. The fact is, that when excess funds are available to individuals or institutions they automatically find their way into investments or speculations of one sort or another, *regardless of value considerations.*

If the outlet is the stock market then prices will continue to rise as long as sufficient new money and credit is made available. But, there is a catch. The higher prices rise the more money is required to sustain the rise. In due course, the increase in inflationary purchasing media begins to level out or turn down. Under such conditions, money must flow out of the stock market (to liquidate other credit obligations) and the stock market will fall to about the same extent that inflationary purchasing media is eliminated.

This principle can be illustrated by an actual example. Assume that a new purchase of 1000 shares of International Business Machines will increase the price two points under normal market conditions. In 1949, only $40,000 was required to produce a rise of this magnitude. *By mid 1965 over $1.5 million was required*. In short, stock prices tend to rise faster during a bull market than does the supply of new money available for investment.

The point is that if the market rises on balance *new* money is responsible. Clearly an investor who sells one stock and buys another with the proceeds from the first sale doesn't contribute in any way to a generally higher price level. The necessary new money (or credit) may come from many sources: Savings, borrowed money, checking accounts, credit balances with brokers from the sale of securities at some earlier date or from liquidation of positions in other markets. But by far, the largest quantity of new purchasing power comes from newly created credit over and above that required to finance the production and distribution of goods and services.

But how and why will stock prices rise so much faster and further than the supply of new credit? Actually, they don't. Instead the market becomes increasingly "selective." Fewer and fewer stocks participate as the rise ripens. For every 100 stocks that gain 10% during the first year of the bull market only 10 stocks will move up by an equivalent amount during the fourth year.

The effect of monetary inflation in the stock market was never more pronounced than between the years 1942–1946. The cost of defense (and offense) spending was translated largely into demand deposits or government obligations such as E bonds, which could be turned into cash on short notice. Moreover, because of war-time restrictions, the normal outlets for these funds such as new business ventures and durable goods purchases were largely lacking. As a result, a sufficient amount of this new purchasing power was funneled into the stock market to produce a surging bull market. Furthermore, a goodly amount of these otherwise idle funds was in the hands of individuals who had no previous market experience. As a result, low priced stocks were bid up to astronomical levels. And while it cannot be proved with figures, that bull market was more all-inclusive and rose much higher than indicated by the popular market averages. Probably more individual issues participated in that rise than at any time since then—and with less reason.

Starting in 1946, and lasting until the spring of 1949, the situation was reversed. A period of monetary *deflation* existed. Despite sharply higher corporate earnings and dividends, money was flowing out of the stock market to finance new business ventures and expansion, the purchase of long deferred durable goods, etc. As a result, stocks declined during these years to the surprise of a majority of observers.

Beginning in the spring of 1949, the Federal Reserve unleashed its "engine of inflation" in an effort to counteract the recession then underway. Massive doses of easy credit were administered. The resulting excess of inflationary purchasing media turned the stock market up in mid-1949. The short-lived business recession turned into a full scale boom when the unexpected Korean War broke out. Inventory speculation and build-ups and a resumption of large scale defense spending occurred. By early 1951, monetary inflation had reached record heights. Here it should be pointed out that a small additional amount of credit provided by the Federal Reserve and Treasury operations can spark a very much greater inflationary credit spiral in the private sector of the economy.

Between 1951 and 1953, the credit brakes were applied and considerable monetary inflation was eliminated. As a result, the stock market declined for two years and the second post-war business recession began in mid-1953. Again the money managers acted swiftly. Early in 1953 the Federal Reserve Banks purchased $1.5 billion of government securities in the open market, reduced reserve requirements by $1.2 billion and reduced margin requirements on stock purchases. All of these steps were highly inflationary and provided the credit for the steep 1954–55 upswing.

The easy money policy was replaced with a policy of restricting credit in 1955 and by mid-1957 most of the inflationary purchasing media created between 1953 and 1955 had been liquidated. As usual the stock market declined by a comparable extent and business activity also turned down.

The same sequence occurred in 1960–1961, and by the mid-1960's credit financed inflation fueled by international tensions had pushed stock prices to all time highs. While periods of inflationary excesses will be partially liquidated in the future as in the past, the plain fact is that today deflation has become politically untenable. Deflation appears to be linked in the minds of ambitious seekers of public office with political suicide.

Thus, we have another sound reason for being 100% invested in UPB stocks as long as the superior profit trend is intact. In the event of a recession, easy money will prevail, interest rates will decline. In short, strong inflationary forces will be unleashed. Whatever happens, the investor is confronted with either boom or inflationary conditions.

But can this go on forever? Won't there be an inevitable day reckoning? We shall now look at the other side of the politically motivated inflation and deficit financing forever theory.

CHAPTER 22

Are Crises Obsolete?

There is a growing conviction in the middle 1960's that we have, at last, found the key to perpetual prosperity; that future recessions will at the worst be mild and quickly reversible. The President's Council of Economic Advisers tells us this is true because of the "New Economics" that prevails and this heightened understanding of the economy will effectively prevent any future depression or deflation.

The least we can do is look at the other side of the coin. And to do this we turn to a recent appraisal of the long-term health of the economy by a Swiss economist Dr. Felix Somary, who accurately predicted the 1929 collapse and ensuing depression *before* it happened. He was a lone voice then, just as he is today.

These partial and slightly revised portions of Dr. Somary's article: "Are Crises Things of the Past," are reproduced with the permission of the American Institute for Economic Research, Great Barrington, Massachusetts.

"We are not, as you know, dealing with a new problem. Around 1900, one looked upon the crisis of 1873, with its destruction of the stock market and total paralysis of

192

economic life, as something dreadful and unique; and it was generally thought that so much experience had been gained thereby as to exclude the possibility of any repetition of such a catastrophe."

"This crisis of 1873 had ended . . . the period of expansion initiated by Napoleon III. In his pamphlet of 1847 he had proclaimed four guiding principles for economic policy; elimination of poverty; the rule of the masses; replacement of the liberal program by the new social program, reducing the claims of the state—the new question being, "what does the state owe me?"; this program to be financed by debts, on the argument that the public debt was not a liability but an asset to the economy. I believe we have recently heard similar arguments propounded as a new theory . . . These were the slogans which preceded the greatest crisis of the 19th century—echoes of the past with a strangely modern ring."

Old Slogans

"The slogans of the late twenties of our century also sound as though written today. I quote them verbatim:

"The stockmarket reflects nothing but technical progress . . . Poverty will disappear from the earth. All that needs to be done is to extend consumption and satisfy the last consumer. One car for every household would not suffice; the goal should be two. One ought to invest one's savings in stocks and never sell them. To provide the inexperienced with opportunities for participation, investment trusts ought to be formed—and in short order no less than 500 appeared. To offer the middle classes opportunities for speculation, stocks were to be split more frequently. To maximize consumption, instalment buying should be indefinitely extended."

"Shortly after the crash, Frederic Lewis Allen humorously described this boom:

"The American envisioned an America set free from poverty and toil. He saw a magical order built on the new science and the new prosperity, airplanes darkening the skies—and smartly dressed men and women, spending, spending, spending with the money they had won by being farsighted enough to foresee, way back in 1929, what was going to happen. The everlasting reiterated phrase of the day was: Conditions are fundamentally sound."

"And some of you would remember the prediction of the Harvard Economic Society of October '29:

"We believe that the slump in stock prices will prove an intermediate movement and not a precursor of a business depression. If recession should threaten serious consequences for business (as is not indicated at present) there is little doubt that the reserve system would take steps to check the movement."

*　*　*　*　*

"In the war sector (of the U. S. economy today), the demand is unlimited, depreciation is rapid, weapons are replaced as soon as one or the other side discovers better ones, the products at times become outdated in the interval between order and delivery. Here the inventive spirit receives unlimited subsidies. More inventions are created and developed within a handful of years that would ordinarily be the case in decades, because progress is not restrained by cost. Official statistics include these products as 'goods' or even 'durable goods'—which is a mistake, since these are not assets but liabilities to the national economy."

"The inventions succeed one another more rapidly than they can be digested by the civilian economy; they provide unique opportunities for businessmen and their workers, but exert a severely destructive effect on the productive system.

"If high military expenditures are indispensable, because they are forced by the opponent, elementary rules of economy would demand that all other expenditures be drastically curtailed. But precisely the opposite is happening. Governments try to hasten the tempo of development in all major areas. Consider, for instance, the immense sum expended on guarantees for veterans' housing—which do not appear on the budget—long-term credit for cheaply built houses extended almost to full value and without real test of credit worthiness. And this is only one of several instances. If one for once were to add up all these extra-budgetary guarantees, I would estimate—and I do not think this is an exaggeration—that they would approach the level of the national debt.

"Even more dangerous to the condition of the market than guarantees and subsidies is the policy of cheap money. Low interest rates drive up the value of securities and the price of real estate. Some singularly impertinent building speculators considered these terms still not sufficiently low; they asserted their 'right' to cheap credit."

"Whence then came this extraordinary expansion of the credit market? Essentially from that part of the national debt from the second world war which had to be taken up on short terms. Today 20 years after the end of the war, none of this debt has been repaid and the attempt to consolidate even 1% thereof has failed. The debt survives under the euphemistic name "treasury bills," typically ever-renewed notes whose redemption can be thought of, if at all, only by the sharpest reduction in the value of money."

"Who today still remembers the time when the Federal Reserve System was created? The notes of that time were issued by banks of the several states, on the basis of their public (not federal) debt; the government, for good reasons, wished to tie the issuance of money to the requirements of trade. Now once again debts, then in such ill repute, have been made the basis of the monetary system; they are a hundred times larger; and they have even found theoretical justification. As the Dutchman, Pinto in the 18th, and Napoleon III in the 19th century, well-known economists of our day regard state debts as an asset to the economy."

"To these treasury bills which have the character of interest-bearing bank notes, we must add a large number of industrial acceptances, for some companies running up to a billion dollars. This form of financing has always been considered especially dangerous, since it shares only the outward form, but not the essence of the commercial note—it is cheap financing without justification.

"We have thus to deal with a money market totally different in character from that of earlier times: indefinitely extended and based upon debts, it is as though one were to build ever higher skyscrapers on a foundation of swamp."

"Hans Freyer, in his theory of the present epoch, came

to a curious result: the surface of the earth has altered more within the past 30 years than in the course of the preceding millions of years. I would not like to say anything so drastic of the current economy, but having presented the analogy of the last crisis, I must point to certain changes which have barely penetrated the consciousness of our contemporaries."

"Already in earlier cycles, the various interests in favor of a bullish market formed a sizable group: among them were the businessmen, the trade unions, the majority of traders and above all, the debtors."

"Here we have a paradox: one would think that the volume of debts grows in a depression and declines when business is good; but in reality precisely the opposite is true because—the upswing constantly increases the tension between interest rates and anticipated profits. Stock market debt, construction debt, consumer debt—they create a frighteningly large group interested in the depreciation of money."

"Vis-a-vis these interests the state used to protect the value of money; the English century-old tradition of honest money gradually came to be shared by all. By its side stood the owners of great and the managers of modest fortunes—insurance, saving and pension banks—furthermore, the independent middle classes and farmers."

"With the exception of the two last named, the situation is now altered: all others have moved into the camp of the speculator, with the state leading the way."

"In contrast with England, the leading power in the world today lacks the tradition of stable money. Strange as it may sound, here debtors were in the overwhelming majority already in the 18th century, and their preponderance today is greater than ever. And the federal government, still almost free of debt at the turn of this century, now carries a gigantic burden, sharing thereby the interest of all debtors. Occasionally one hears, here and there, official reassurances to the contrary—unfortunately mere words which contradict reality."

"Stable currency has thereby lost its strongest support. Jobbery and inflation have shed their age-old ill repute and become respectable. And a good proportion of the scientific gentlemen have adapted their theory to the prevailing climate. The tax structure, moreover, has led even the big capitalist to shift sides.

"The federal income tax leaves the owner of an income up to $100,000 only $25,000. Investment funds for the most part can therefore be drawn only from corporate surplus and from financial institutions; the individual capitalist, however, is dependent on capital gains as a source for investment funds as well as for any increase of income and property. If this source dries up, his income will yield him no more than a small commission for living expenses."

"This adds a new element of rigidity to the economy: besides wages, which allegedly may only be raised, but never lowered, we now have capital gains. They represent almost the last remnant of individual capitalism. Within the span of barely a generation, the income tax has already been exploited to its outermost limit."

"The state and the individual, employer and employee, are committed to perpetual inflation; parliaments and governments obey them. The government must prevent crises; it must guarantee economic stability—and beyond that, guarantee full employment; but even this is not enough: it must concern itself with perpetual prosperity.

It must do it, it can do it, therefore, it shall do it."

"These are the slogans of our day. There is but scant difference between East and West as regards faith in the omniscience and omnipotence of the state. Freed of all pretense, the program means simply; economic stability at the cost of monetary instability. And since slumps are taboo, inflation is the fashion of the day."

"It is currently proper to accuse the men of 1930 of inadequate skill in handling the monetary system and to claim that with the knowledge we have today, they could have avoided the crisis. A small inflationary infusion, it is held, is all that is required to master any situation. In the 30's, it is said, they were overly frightened of inflation and did not understand how to administer it.

"I have no reason to defend the governments of those days; but the accusation is as unfounded as is, unfortunately, the degree of confidence shown in their successors."

"The European continent knew the price of inflation all too well. It had created Bolshevism in Russia, and Lenin bragged that Communism would not have to wage war, since inflation by itself would finish the task of destruction. As was still all too fresh in memory, it had destroyed the bourgeoisie of three great continental nations. To Englishmen and Americans, who would not acknowledge the relevance of other people's experience, inflation could be presented as a panacea; but not to people who had so recently experienced the painful blessings of permanent monetary devaluation. They rejected this nostrum not from ignorance but from all too thorough familiarity. That this "raging plague," as Mirabeau called it has now also invaded the country of all our hopes, is among the most painful of our experiences."

"In America, several objections will be raised against this view:

"(a) On the one hand there are those who deny the fact of inflation, by pointing to the stability of food prices. The same thing happened in 1928. Numerous branches of agriculture cannot keep up with the rapid development of all industry, particularly of the war sector. This is due not only to obvious technical reasons, but rather to what may at first seem like a paradox, the demand for agricultural goods is limited by the purchasing power of the population; the demand for war goods is in principle unlimited. One is determined by an economic calculus, the other is not. For the second time in one generation the farmer—on both sides of the iron curtain—is being made the victim of prosperity. This contains the seeds of crisis, not of strength."

"Capital goods are of infinitely greater importance than consumption goods. And here prices have risen fantastically, with a very short time span.

"(b) On the other side, the fact of inflation is met by the argument that production is growing proportionately. But this calculation includes military equipment in total output—and this, as has already been stated, is not an economic good. What is important is not really production itself, but the salability of goods—surely two crucially different things. But even if, for purposes of simplification, we take production increases as the basis, we must still contrast them with security values in order to measure inflation."

"In a typical post-war year American production rose by 7%; after military equipment has been subtracted, by roughly 5½%. In the same period the prices of stocks listed on the New York Stock Exchange, exclusive of preferred shares, rose by no less than 24%. This cannot be explained merely by a transfer of holdings from cash to securities or an exchange of bonds for equity. Here, at the most sensitive juncture, the inflationary effect is unmistakable."

"(c) Two other groups admit the existence of inflation, but declare it to be harmless, or even useful. One group says that in light of America's ruling position, it can afford inflation without any danger; the other group suggests that the government can always invoke measures to control it."

"In other countries, inflation means that the international value of their currency will slip—but this is held to be impossible in the case of America. Vis-a-vis which country could the dollar possibly incur a discount? In Switzerland, the only country which could come in question, the export interests would doom any such attempt to failure."

"This is why, this group argues, the American Government can calmly intervene with inflationary money at any threat of an economic setback; the boom can be stemmed or the retrenchment avoided by a few simple steps . . . How marvelously different is this (so say the proponents of this doctrine) from the 'dark ages'—those barbaric times like 1929 or 1907, when the rate for call money rose to 20% or even 100%."

"Above all, however, according to this view, the government now knows how to manage the economy—by wage increases, subsidies and guarantees—so that no one need suffer the consequences of inflation."

"But if this were true, one would not have to initiate an inflation. Its effect, after all, rests on the more or less complete expropriation of several large groups."

"Whether or not the balance of payments position is indeed unshakable, only the future will show. But in light of America's leading political position, it can never be too strong. It has generally escaped attention that Switzerland, Holland and West Germany together, with only 40% of America's population have more gold than America."

"(d) The fifth group, which can be described as the realists, is the most extensive one. They frankly admit the existence of inflation, and do not concern themselves with whether it is a blessing or a curse, since they consider it unavoidable. It is popular and easy, they argue, to initiate an inflation; it is difficult and unpopular to apply the brakes. It had been thought that the Republicans would do it, but the hope was disappointed; both parties will continue to create money by this simple device. The inflation will run its course, precisely as elsewhere, but in America it will take longer. (Men of 70 like to give it 10; men of 60, 20; and men of 50, 30 years, since they can envision but would not like to see the bitter end.)

"The policy of this group is to liquidate cash and bond holdings; to invest capital in ventures and stocks; to borrow extensively with the intent to liquidate these debts in devalued money; in short, to adopt the entire range of practices all too well known in Vienna, London and especially Paris."

"To him who foresees perpetual devaluation of money, no rate is too high. The adherents of this group contribute decisively to the increase in money velocity, because they are afraid of money; as soon as any comes into their hands, they are in frantic haste to invest it; and even more rapidly they invest all borrowed funds. As is generally known, borrowed money has the highest velocity of circulation."

"This group is not generally prone to express its thoughts in public, but it is quite extensive and until now it has met with considerable success. Great fortunes have been made quite rapidly, and the circle of adherents has increased many times. It is undeniable that the men of this persuasion can argue a strong case; large groups in the country are enjoying the inflation; even in the face of a strong enemy, they would like to celebrate, and it takes considerable courage to wrest them from their illusions back to the grim reality."

"One cannot trust the government to show such courage—and we may express the same doubt as regards many governments other than the American."

"In Europe, 45 years ago, I waged an active battle against several governments in which I advocated immediate and drastic anti-inflationary measures. Their counter-arguments were hardly convincing—for the real basis of their opposition lay elsewhere. Such measures have to be carried through and the responsibility for them must be taken by the government of the day, but the final consequences of the inflation are chalked up on the successors' slate. Such motivations are particularly strong in election years."

"It goes without saying that no government will admit to the actual state of affairs; and generally any attempt to invoke brakes will be met with a comment about the dangers of Communism."

"But why, ask the optimists, should one bring on the crisis precisely from fear of crisis? Is not inflation preferable so long as one knows how to manipulate it so precisely that one need feel only its pleasant effects? And could not America extend the inflationary state to 1980, as Professor Baudouin believes, or to the Day of Judgment as Mr. Slichter predicted?"

"Such a policy recommends itself by its popularity; whosoever goes against the current will end as a martyr—and nowhere on earth is there less inclination to such a role than in America. Therefore, why not permit things to go on as they do, since everything seems to be in such good order? The political situation, it is commonly thought, will not change in any event; it seems likely that for a long time to come one will continue to prepare for a war that will in fact never be waged. The situation therefore, is thought more secure than in any previous period of prosperity. This, in sum, seems to be the public opinion of our day."

"But is it, I ask, an advantage to have prosperity determined by political rather than economic elements? Can its development be predicted more easily when it hinges on decisions of a few individuals whom nobody really knows?"

"To start an inflation is easy, to stop it is immensely difficult, particularly for a democracy. One may quarrel about whether it is a permissible remedy for all but the most drastic emergencies; but it is difficult to believe that it ever has been permitted to rule with as little justification as at present."

"Since, however, a healthy currency is no less important for waging war than are modern armaments, the American Government cannot afford to let the currency run down; it has to interfere before wide circles are gripped by a loss of confidence. The later this happens, the higher the price that will be exacted for the protection of sound currency—and I fear that even today it would be quite high enough."

"Now you will doubtless ask me: is a crisis unavoidable?"

"Under the given circumstances: Yes!"

"Not, of course, as the Marxists claim, because it lies in the nature of the capitalist system."

"It could be avoided, on one indispensable condition:

"That the government renounces its fears of the public and finds the courage to express and act upon its convictions. This, in the democracies of our time, seems to me no longer possible."

"(a) The arrogance of the employers and the trade union leaders' greed increases with each inflationary wave; both permit themselves to be carried along comfortably by ever more rapid currents, without giving a thought to the end."

"(b) The governments are but obedient slaves of the "Inflationists"; at each new step they call out, just like the nursemaid to the baby, 'only once more and that's all.' "

"(c) Out of a baseless fear of communism, the serious danger of the situation is being thoughtlessly accelerated, while every attempt to reverse the trend in time is sabotaged."

"(d) An impolitic demand for full employment has been elevated to a tenet of economic theory. This is the case today not only in America, but America leads the West."

Resume

"The system of cheap money must be totally renounced. The rates for borrowing money should be based on the real rate of interest."

"There should be no borrowing for the purchase of securities."

"The inflation is veiling a fact: that America is living beyond its means. That the same holds true for Russia is no justification for American economic policy, Respice finem!"

"One often tells me that my diagnosis conflicts with the optimism of almost all professional business cycle experts."

"That was also true 35 years ago. Was the crisis predicted by Mitchell, Schumpeter, Spiethoff, Irving Fisher? Of Keynes, his biographer tells us he did foresee it; but in a conversation with me as late as 1928, Keynes emphatically expressed the contrary conviction."

"Be reminded of Anatole France's monk, who is so pleasantly absorbed in the stories of invasions that he does not notice that his cloister has just been invaded by barbarians."

"Crises come precisely when—and because—the mass of men will not believe in them."

CHAPTER 23

The Next Twenty Years

And now to confirm the foolishness of Homo Sapiens:
After ridiculing market seers we shall now take a look at
the future which will, doubtless, prove to be as futile as
most past performances. Nevertheless, some effort must
be made to determine how to protect your capital under
conditions of war, inflation, deflation or depression.
There are four broad future possibilities:

(1) The next 20 years may duplicate the past 20
years. Since World War 2, we have experienced a cold
war which warmed up from time to time, mild recessions,
credit expansion—both public and private, and monetary
inflation (i.e. deficit financing). Chances are the same
pattern will prevail at least during the first part of the next
20 years.

(2) A flight from the dollar will develop, due to a
speeding of inflation and fear of still more inflation. In
fact, the post war rise in real estate and stock prices has
been fueled by these inflation created funds and to some
extent a flight from the dollar has been underway for the
last 20 years. More recently, this has been demonstrated
by the accelerating exchange of dollars for gold by foreign
central banks.

(3) The vast pyramid of credit will collapse precisely

as it collapsed in 1929–1932 and for similar reasons. This, of course, would trigger a comparable collapse in the stock market which would wipe out most of the post-war rise in stock prices.

(4) There will be a full-scale nuclear war. (We rule out this possibility on the assumption that Providence will prevent mankind from commiting this ultimate act of depravity).

Conclusion: Steps 1, 2 & 3 will be experienced in the order listed. We do not presume to predict when or with what degree of severity each will be experienced but we do think farsighted investors should plan to protect the purchasing power of their capital under all three conditions.

The best protection against inflation is to increase your income at a faster rate than the inflation is growing. The next best hedge is to own several UPB stocks. Stock market history reveals repeatedly that such stocks rise at a much faster rate than any inflation.

But, if there is going to be a depression, when should these stocks be sold? Answer: when the UPB factor no longer applies. By applying this yardstick you will gradually but automatically eliminate those stocks that will prove vulnerable to a severe business depression and a severe stock market decline.

But you should hold UPB stocks indefinitely as long as their earnings continue to rise at a unique rate regardless of the trend of "the market" *or of other stocks or of the price trend of the stocks you still own.* Here you may ask with ample justification; "but won't even a UPB stock decline drastically during a bear market?" The answer, of course, is yes. But we have already documented the futility of trying to time a market top. The point is: UPB stocks will decline much less than the average stock and when the bear market runs its course, or even before, they will quickly rebound to new highs.

To illustrate, in the early 1930's many gold stocks proved to be ideal UPB issues. Homestake for one, fell from 92 to 65 in the 1929 crash, but passed 100 early in 1931 and subsequently passed 500. And the initial stages of this rise occurred long before the dollar was devalued. As early as 1930 net income turned up strongly as labor and other costs turned down.

Still another UPB example from that era was the emergence of talking pictures as the nation's favorite amusement. Loew's, for instance, boosted earnings from $7.91 in 1929, to $9.65 in 1930 and the stock moved from a low of 32 in 1929 to a high of 98 in 1930. Those who sold before the crash made a serious mistake.

More recently, in the 1962 bear market, Xerox—a prime example of a UPB company—was cut in half—from 34 to 17, then it surged to above 140. Those who sold in anticipation of the 1962 market crash made a costly mistake. The guiding principle was that Xerox was (and still is as this is written) still a UPB company and so should have been held. Thus, between 1962 and 1964 net income rose 165%, which certainly represents a UNIQUE PROFIT BREAKTHROUGH.

How else to hedge against the perils that will undoubtedly be encountered in the next 20 years? Without much doubt, and especially if an economic depression is the end result of the inevitable credit crisis and panic, the dollar will be devalued. The best hedge against devaluation will be gold stocks. And gold stocks will be an ideal hedge against deflation even if not accompanied by an increase in the price of gold.

Another hedge is to hold silver coins. The dimes, quarters and halves now in circulation contain 93% pure silver, so that 10 dimes, 2 quarters or any half dollar contains 47 cents worth of pure silver. Undoubtedly, if the price of gold is raised, a similar increase will occur in the price of silver. In fact, there is a good chance the price of silver will rise above its monetary pegged level of $1.293 an ounce even without a change in the price of gold. Certainly, few comparable investments, i.e. diamonds and the like, have the universal acceptability of silver coins. Since about 750 B.C. silver coins have been readily and universally accepted in exchange for goods when base metal coins and paper money were not accepted.

A small portion of your assets should also be held in cash in a safety deposit box as a hedge against future bank holidays and in Federally insured bank savings accounts. For a number of reasons, beyond the scope of this book, we counsel against any investment in Savings and Loan deposits.

Why hold cash or its equivalent during a period when a runaway inflation might render the cash virtually worthless? The catch here is "might." Who can rule out the possibility that a credit liquidation panic might occur after only a modest additional amount of inflating takes place? History shows that those who have cash when others need it desperately can make very large profits in a short time and with very little risk.

DATE DUE
